THE ULTIMATE TRIVIA GAME BOOK FOR ADULTS

975 Trivia Questions Across 13 Super Fun Quiz Categories for Game Night or Solo Play

BILL O'NEILL

ISBN: 978-1-64845-126-3

CONTENTS

INTRODUCTION

This isn't just a book of quippy little facts.

The Ultimate Trivia Game Book for Adults has so much more to offer than just boring questions and answers. This book is for the true trivia enthusiast, whether you're a veteran quizmaster or a novice just looking for a way to spice up a game night. In these pages, you'll find snappy questions and interesting factoids that are sure to entertain you and others.

Take a journey through history, dabble in the arts, or get lost in spy plots in this book. With 13 chapters that cover a breadth of subjects, eras, and places, there's sure to be something for everyone - and who knows, you might just want to dive in on your own! It's pretty safe to say that once you get started, you won't want to stop.

Here's your first bit of trivia, on the house: Trivia games can help sharpen memory and improve cognitive function, so not only is it fun, but it's also good for you! It's so much more than just knowing what the capital of the state of Washington is, or how much an elephant would weigh on Jupiter. Trivia can be a fun and interesting way to get a glimpse of our interesting and diverse world (and beyond) from the comfort of your own home.

With so much easy information at our fingertips through smartphones, tablets, and laptops, this book can provide a real test of not just your knowledge, but your ability to retain new information too. Challenge yourself, make a trivia team, or host a trivia night with the rules and play styles set out at the beginning of the book. It's meant to be flexible and easy to use, so don't hesitate to adapt the rules to your needs. And above all, have fun!

HOW TO PLAY

There are several different ways that this book can be used (and probably many more we haven't thought of - don't hesitate to get creative!) These are just some basic rules for the simplest play styles.

Each chapter is divided into sections that deal with a specific aspect of the subject of that chapter. Within these sections, there are two styles of trivia questions: true/false and multiple choice. The true/ false ones will be the easiest to answer, multiple choice being a bit more difficult. This is simply due to the nature of answering them, not necessarily a reflection of the subjects they cover.

Single

Test yourself! You can pick a set number of questions, either from one chapter or many, and then write down your answers. Check your answers when you're done. For an added challenge, time yourself! See how long it takes you to answer, and then try to beat your best time, or see how many you can answer within a time limit. For the most difficult challenge, close your eyes, flip to a random page, and then answer the questions there, so it's a surprise.

Pair

Take turns quizzing each other, either out loud or by writing down your answers as above. For an extra challenge, try a lightning round of fast, rapid-fire questions from one or more chapters.

Group

Divide the players into two or more teams. Designate one person as the "Quiz Master" who will oversee asking the questions and looking up the answers. Teams can answer collectively, or each member can take a turn answering a question individually. Keep score and use a timer for an added challenge.

Survivor Mode

If a player answers a question incorrectly, they will be removed from the team. Keep score based on teams, not individuals. Alternatively, the team with the highest score can vote to remove a player from the team with the lowest score. The last team standing is the winner!

CHAPTER 1:
ANCIENT HISTORY

ASIA

TRUE OR FALSE

1. In addition to wielding a variety of swords, Japanese samurai were accomplished gun users.
2. Renowned Shang dynasty general Fu Hao was a royal consort.
3. The first kingdom on the Korean peninsula was known as the Kim Kingdom.
4. In 939 CE, the area that would later become Vietnam won independence from Japan.
5. Beginning in the 1st century CE, Malaysia adopted Hinduism and Buddhism due to contact with traders from France and China.
6. The first written mention of Japan in history is in the Chinese *Book of Han*.
7. The Jōmon people were the first inhabitants of Japan.
8. The first emperor of China was King Zheng of Qin, who would go on to inspire the name "China."
9. The "Java Man," a *Homo erectus* fossil discovered in the 1800s, is so named because of the dark brown color of the fossil.
10. The *Vedas* are the oldest scriptures associated with Hinduism.

MULTIPLE CHOICE

1. Under Tokugawa Ieyasu's influence, Japan adopted a policy of *Sakoku,* which meant:

A. Trade could only be organized under the auspices of the Emperor's office
B. Japan would adopt a policy of isolationism, meant to limit the influence of foreigners
C. Samurai would be forced to adopt a strict code of conduct
D. All other lands in East Asia were to be conquered and brought under Japanese control, as they were the only ones worthy of ruling

2. The first Chinese dynasty, for which there is conflicting evidence, was known as:

A. The Qing
B. The Yao
C. The Great Dragon
D. The Xia

3. The Yayoi people, who would go on to mingle with or overtake the Jōmon people, settled in the Japanese islands and originated from where?

A. The Korean peninsula
B. China's east coast region
C. Modern-day Indonesia
D. The northern part of Laos

4. The extensive trade route that allowed Taiwanese green and white nephrite to be traded and worked among several different peoples was known as:

A. The Jade Exchange
B. The Eastern Sea Lane
C. The Maritime Jade Road
D. The Emperor's Path

5. Which nation was home to a unique species of ancient hominins, which were likely pygmies, known as *Homo luzonensis*?

A. Indonesia
B. Malaysia
C. The Philippines
D. Korea

ROME

TRUE OR FALSE

1. Garum is a sauce made from fermented fish that was popular throughout Rome and even touted as a health cure.
2. The Roman Empire had public schools for all children, inspiring other cultures that took their cues from ancient Rome.
3. Advanced education was necessary to enter a career in politics.
4. The toga, and how it was decorated, could display the wearer's social standing.
5. Romans only wore sandals, believing that other forms of shoes were unnecessarily decadent.
6. Like much of their society, early Roman literature was heavily influenced by the Greeks.
7. An early Roman art style was painting indoor areas to look like marble.
8. Roman musical performances were reserved for military parades.
9. Though originally built for horses and foot traffic, some roads constructed by the Romans are still in use today.
10. The Romans banned the local religions in all areas they conquered.

MULTIPLE CHOICE

1. When the Roman Empire began to crumble in the 5th century CE, the eastern half of the empire persisted and became later known as the:

A. Holy Roman Empire
B. *Remnus Persistae*
C. Romulans
D. Byzantine Empire

2. What is the 200 years of peace that began with Octavian Augusts Caesar's rule known as, given that any attempts at rebellion from the provinces were dealt with via shocking brutality?

A. *Pax per Violentiam*
B. *Sanguis et Pax*
C. *Pax Romana*
D. *Pax per Regula*

3. Whether or not a Roman was considered free (*liberi*) or a slave (*servi*) was determined at birth by:

A. Their father's status
B. Their mother's status
C. The status of the family as a whole
D. Their father's service record

4. The famous Roman art and games were largely funded through:

A. Private citizens in order to justify their wealth and status
B. Heavy taxes on the provinces
C. Public fundraising that was seen as the duty of every citizen
D. Ticket sales to said games

5. *Virtus*, or "valor," was the predominant concept regarding Roman men's sexuality for much of the history of the Empire, which in practice meant:

A. Men were restricted to only engaging in sex for procreation
B. Engaging in sex outside of marriage was punishable by law for married men
C. Men should only desire women
D. Men could be attracted to either sex, so long as they were the ones doing the penetrating

AMERICAS

TRUE OR FALSE

1. For the Aztecs, it was much more important to capture enemies to sacrifice than it was to kill them.
2. The Mayan civilization was egalitarian, with everyone owning property communally.
3. Horses had never lived in the Americas until European contact.
4. The people of Mesoamerica had no armor that they wore into battle.
5. Many people in North and South America were gifted astronomers.
6. Guinea pigs were a common source of food for the people of South America.
7. The Constitution of the United States is based on an agreement called the Iroquois Confederacy.
8. There were no large-scale cities in North America until European colonization.
9. Corn was a naturally occurring food that the Native Americans took advantage of.
10. All Native Americans in North America lived in tipis.

MULTIPLE CHOICE

1. The first complex civilization in Mesoamerica was:

A. The Mayan
B. The Inca
C. The Aztec
D. The Olmec

2. The famous text that was transcribed from Mayan hieroglyphics and details their religion and history is known as the:

A. *Words of Kukulkan*
B. *K'iche Cycle*
C. *Popol Vuh*
D. Hun Hunahpu

3. Which massive city in the central United States near what is now St. Louis, Missouri, was home to as many as 15,000 people?

A. Tenochtitlan
B. Cahokia
C. Chaco
D. Machu Picchu

4. During the Paleoindian period, which group, noted for their distinct spear-tip designs, exported or traded their unique weapons across North America from Canada to Mexico?

A. Clovis culture
B. Pueblo-builders
C. Suwannee
D. Proto-Dryas

5. The South American people that provide the foundation for the myth of *El Dorado*, or the City of Gold, were the:

A. Inca
B. Bogota
C. Muisca
D. Nahuatl

EGYPT

TRUE OR FALSE

1. Despite her connections to famous Roman generals, Cleopatra never visited Rome.
2. Egyptian workers were usually paid in grain and beer instead of actual wages.
3. The people that built the Great Pyramid were highly skilled workers and not slaves.
4. Egyptian walls were painted with a pigment made from ground minerals and honey.
5. In ancient Egypt, the heart was considered to be where thoughts were formed rather than the brain.
6. After death, the Egyptians believed that their hearts would be weighed on a scale against a grain of rice to determine if they were worthy of passing to the afterlife.
7. Wine was the drink of choice for Egyptians, who preferred it above all else.
8. Egyptian doctors were highly specialized and renowned throughout the ancient world.
9. Kissing was depicted in art (and likely done in person) by rubbing noses together.
10. The god Osiris is commonly depicted with golden skin as a reflection of his divine nature.

MULTIPLE CHOICE

1. What was the name of the last dynasty in ancient Egypt, named for the general under Alexander the Great who established the line?

A. Macedonic
B. Ptolemaic
C. Intermedic
D. Archaic

2. The containers in which the organs that were removed during mummification were stored are known as:

A. Anubis jars
B. Duat chests
C. Dessicationus
D. Canopic jars

3. Which of these is not one of four recognized female pharaohs, who ruled solely and not in conjunction with a male pharaoh?

A. Hatshepsut
B. Neferneferuaten
C. Merneith
D. Sobekneferu

4. The concept of the pharaoh's responsibility for maintaining balance through order and laws shared the name of a goddess known as:

A. Isis
B. Ma'at
C. Bennu
D. Ba-res

5. The estate of a nobleman or a temple could have its prestige and prosperity determined by the number of which livestock they owned, considered the most important and with religious significance?

A. Cattle
B. Sheep
C. Horses
D. Goats

MESOPOTAMIA

TRUE OR FALSE

1. Current-day Afghanistan is part of ancient Mesopotamia.
2. The first city in the area was Uruk.
3. Mesopotamia is also known as "The Fertile Triangle."
4. All of the preserved writing from this period is on clay tablets.
5. Mesopotamian mathematics used a base-60 number system.
6. The Mesopotamians were famous for their steel and iron works.
7. The oldest Mesopotamian medical texts are over 4,500 years old.
8. Temples functioned as banks.
9. Mesopotamian art is heavily focused on painting.
10. In the city of Ur, most people were buried under the house where they had lived.

MULTIPLE CHOICE

1. The one-time enemy and later companion and comrade of Gilgamesh, the ruler and protagonist of *The Epic of Gilgamesh*, was known as:

A. Enkidu
B. Humbaba
C. Babyl
D. Urku

2. The Mesopotamians believed that all life, including Earth itself, was born from:

A. A giant flaming bull
B. A rock that split open to reveal the living world in one half, and the Underworld or realm of the dead in the other.
C. A vast, limitless sea
D. The union between a primordial goddess and the concept of Time

3. A form of polo was a popular sport in Mesopotamia, but instead of riding on horses, men would ride:

A. On the shoulders of other men
B. Camels
C. Bulls
D. Small chariots pulled by goats

4. Women in Mesopotamia had the right to:

A. Own property
B. Hold public office
C. Divorce their husbands with sufficient reason
D. Both A and C

5. The thriving Mesopotamian civilization established an early and fruitful trading partnership with which other civilization?

A. Hittite
B. Indus Valley
C. Euphratean
D. Assyrian

ANSWER KEYS:

Asia

TRUE OR FALSE

1. True
2. True
3. False. It was called Gojoseon.
4. True
5. False. At that time there was no contact between what would become France and any part of Asia.
6. True
7. True
8. True
9. False. It was named for the Java Island where it was discovered.
10. True

MULTIPLE CHOICE

1. B
2. D
3. A
4. C
5. C

Rome

TRUE OR FALSE

1. True
2. False. The head of each household decided what education each member should have.
3. True
4. True
5. False. A variety of footwear was used for different occasions.
6. True
7. True
8. False. Rome had street musicians, and music was a large part of everyone's day.
9. True
10. False. They allowed local religion to flourish, as long as the Roman pantheon was also worshiped, with the two frequently merging over time.

MULTIPLE CHOICE

1. D
2. C
3. B
4. A
5. D

Americas

TRUE OR FALSE

1. True
2. False. The Mayans had a very stratified society, with a great separation between the nobility and commoners.
3. False. Horses roamed the continent long before Europeans arrived but were hunted to extinction.
4. False. They used armor made of layers of cotton, obsidian, and leather.
5. True
6. True
7. True
8. False. Some natives were prolific city builders, and there were large stone cities.
9. False. Corn was extensively farmed and purpose grown.
10. False. Permanent buildings of wood and stone were common in some areas.

MULTIPLE CHOICE

1. D
2. C
3. B
4. A
5. C

Egypt

TRUE OR FALSE

1. False. Much like rulers today, Cleopatra went on state visits, and the Romans seemed greatly confused by her, to put it mildly.
2. True
3. True

4. False. Milk was the most common base ingredient for paints, used to provide brilliant colors that lasted a long time.
5. True
6. False. It was weighed against a feather.
7. False. A porridge-like beer was the daily drink of choice.
8. True
9. True
10. False. It was commonly green or blue to denote his undead status.

MULTIPLE CHOICE

1. B
2. D
3. C
4. B
5. A

Mesopotamia

TRUE OR FALSE

1. False. Afghanistan is just outside of the Mesopotamian area.
2. True
3. False. It was known as the "Fertile Crescent."
4. True
5. True
6. False. Their bronze works were great, however.
7. True
8. True
9. False. Sculpture was the main means of their artistic expression.
10. True

MULTIPLE CHOICE

1. A
2. C
3. A
4. D
5. B

CHAPTER 2:
FOOD

SWEET THINGS

TRUE OR FALSE

1. Sweet desserts were fed to the gods in ancient India.
2. Sugarcane was common in Europe in 500 BCE.
3. The first published apple pie recipe is from 1381.
4. Chocolate, in the form of cacao beans, was used as currency in Mesoamerica.
5. A common dessert in the medieval period was candied pigs' feet.
6. Afghan biscuits are a common dessert in New Zealand.
7. Danishes are called "Vienna Breads" in Denmark.
8. Boba tea originated in Taiwan in the 1980s.
9. Henry VIII was so fond of candy and dessert that he had a special dessert chef imported from the Middle East.
10. Frozen desserts were served in Persia as early as 500 BCE.

MULTIPLE CHOICE

1. Cookies were introduced to Europe by the:

A. Opening of trade between Portugal and Japan in the 16th century
B. Muslim conquest of Spain
C. Columbian exchange
D. Establishment of a safe trade route through the Ottoman Empire

2. Which of the following are *not* ingredients in a traditional egg cream?

A. Cherries
B. Eggs
C. Cream
D. All of the above

3. The first restaurant to serve a slushy/slurpee after an equipment malfunction in 1958 was:

A. Dairy Queen
B. McDonald's
C. Sonic
D. A&W Rootbeer Stand

4. The word "taffy," the name for the boiled and stretched candy famous in the United States, was first mentioned in 1817, but could also be confusingly used to refer to:

A. A horse that had gone lame
B. Sarcastic or insincere flattery
C. The color of a washer-woman's hair from standing in the sun
D. A desert made of melted butter, sugar, and aspic

5. The original name for Reese's peanut butter cups was:

A. Bullseyes
B. Hoofers
C. Penny cups
D. Nickel-dimes

SPICE IT UP

TRUE OR FALSE

1. Curry needs very specific spicing to be an actual curry.
2. Cinnamon is a common spice for lamb.
3. India produces three times as much spices as the rest of the top ten global producers combined.
4. During the 19th century, it was considered a bad idea for women to eat food that was too spicy because it was believed to be unhealthy for them.
5. The Romans detested saffron and believed it was a sign of bad luck.
6. In the medieval period, spices were used to preserve food.
7. In 2023, the world's hottest pepper, the Carolina Reaper, was dethroned by Pepper X, produced by the same farmer.
8. Pepper plants have been part of South American food for over 9,000 years.
9. King Louis XVI of France attempted to use black pepper to cure his ongoing bedroom woes.
10. In ancient China, emperors were commonly buried with a clove of garlic for luck on their journey to the afterlife.

MULTIPLE CHOICE

1. Despite its association with Louisiana and Cajun cuisine, the tabasco pepper, from which Tabasco sauce is made, originate in:

A. Florida
B. Mexico
C. Southeast China
D. California

2. Though chilis originated in Central and South America, today the largest grower of chilis is:

A. China
B. The United States
C. South Africa
D. India

3. Before trade was established with the New World and the spices and peppers grown there became more readily available, most European dishes (dated back to ancient Greece) were given heat through:

A. Black pepper
B. Long pepper
C. Black garlic
D. Both A and B

4. In ancient Egypt, what was frequently used as a preservative in the process of mummification?

A. Caraway seeds
B. Salted rose petals
C. Cumin
D. Black pepper

5. Which flavoring had unknown origins in Medieval Europe and was sometimes believed to be fished out of the sea using nets?

A. Cinnamon
B. Cardamom
C. Vanilla
D. Turmeric

UNUSUAL FOODS

TRUE OR FALSE

1. While insects are a regular food in many parts of the world, nobody eats cockroaches.
2. Rocky Mountain oysters are actually bull testicles.
3. The state food of Louisiana is alligator gumbo.
4. The cockentrice, a popular medieval food, was the front half of a pig sewn to the back half of a calf.
5. During the 18th century, wealthy women in France would sometimes consume wolf blood to help promote fertility.
6. Romans ate dormice and thought they were delicious.
7. Eels were used as currency in the Middle Ages.
8. Beaver tails were a popular food during Lent because beavers were considered a vegetable.
9. The Swedish delicacy *surströmming* is herring fermented in lactic acid that can explode if left in the can too long.
10. Isinglass jelly was a popular food in the Victorian era, with people frequently putting it on toast.

MULTIPLE CHOICE

1. In Cambodia, it's possible to get a snack of fried 'what' from street vendors?

A. Tarantulas
B. Octopus beak
C. Manta ray
D. Elephant tail

2. *Casu martzu* is made by slicing open pecorino cheese and:

A. Leaving it to age in the sun at low temperatures so that it forms a new rind that is partially rotten
B. Letting it soak in the sea to promote a salty flavor
C. Allowing maggots to grow on it so that they will eat some of the fat and promote fermentation
D. Burying it for a minimum of two years so that it will slowly rot just enough to promote the flavor

3. Silkworm larva, frequently sold in cans, is a common snack in:

A. Japan
B. South Korea
C. Vietnam
D. Guam

4. Chinese century eggs are made by preserving eggs for months at a time in a mixture of:

A. Straw and horse dung
B. Seaweed and coal ashes
C. Dirt and volcanic rock
D. Ash and clay

5. Hawaii consumes the highest amount of Spam every year, totaling how many cans per year?

A. Seven million
B. Five million
C. Three million
D. One million

TABLE MANNERS

TRUE OR FALSE

1. The oldest known mention of table manners is from 200 BCE.
2. Traditional dining in India takes place on the floor with comfortable mats for food and guests to sit on.
3. It is considered polite to compliment the cooking by loudly smacking your lips while eating in South Korea.
4. In China, it is rude to take the last piece of food without it being offered to you.
5. During the rule of King George IV, it was acceptable to use the tablecloth as a napkin.
6. Queen Victoria was a notoriously slow eater, with dinners lasting hours and the guests unable to leave before she was finished.
7. In Korea, it is poor manners to start a meal before expressing how much you expect to enjoy the food.
8. North American 19th-century etiquette states that a spoon should never be pulled toward you when eating soup.
9. In the Medieval period, knives were the only cutlery that was provided.
10. During World War II, metal was in such short supply that it was common to use bread as a spoon due to a flatware shortage.

MULTIPLE CHOICE

1. In which country it is considered bad manners to eat with a fork in your right hand?

A. Australia
B. Austria
C. Russia
D. Mongolia

2. In Italy, it's considered rude to ask for extra 'what' if not offered?

A. Wine
B. Pasta
C. Cheese
D. Napkins

3. It's considered a great compliment to the chef to belch in:

A. Turkey
B. Portugal
C. Scotland
D. China

4. When dining in Russia, it's a sign of disrespect to rest your hands:

A. In your lap
B. On the edge of the table
C. At the sides of your plate
D. Under your chin

5. In Bulgaria, it's inadvisable to bring yellow flowers to your host, as they mean:

A. "I want to sleep with you"
B. "I hate you"
C. "I want to apologize"
D. "I am uncomfortable in your home"

FAST FOOD

TRUE OR FALSE

1. The original side commonly served with fast food sandwiches was beans, not fries.
2. Fast food was commonplace in ancient Rome, and vendors were often frequented by the working class and servants.
3. In the US, fast food corporations spend over five billion dollars each year on advertisements.
4. Taco Bell is named for the famous bell featured prominently on many Spanish missions in the American southwest.
5. It was common for miners in the American West to pull their horses right up to a saloon and order lunch, which served as later inspiration for the drive thru.
6. The first restaurant to serve fish and chips in England has been open for business since 1860.
7. Oysters were considered inappropriate for the poor during the 1800s, especially since they were so quick and easy to prepare.
8. The White Castle hamburger franchise is the oldest fast-food chain in the US, opening its first restaurant in 1916.
9. Kentucky Fried Chicken is so named for the style of cooking rather than where it was founded.
10. The original McDonald's mascot was a hamburger-headed chef named "Speedee."

MULTIPLE CHOICE

1. McDonald's is the largest distributor in the world of what?

A. Beef
B. Toys
C. Chicken nuggets
D. Napkins

2. In Japan, Christmas Eve dinner is typically bought from:

A. Street vendors
B. Kentucky Fried Chicken
C. A special McDonald's menu
D. Subway

3. The Classic Cinnabon has how many calories?

A. 890
B. 755
C. 570
D. 630

4. In-n-Out is credited with inventing the first:

A. Single napkin dispenser
B. Plastic straws
C. Lids for disposable cups
D. Two-way ordering speaker system

5. Which was the first fast food restaurant to offer dining rooms with indoor seating?

A. McDonald's
B. Chick-fil-A
C. Burger King
D. Pizza Hut

ANSWER KEYS:

Sweet Things

TRUE OR FALSE

1. True
2. False. Sugarcane was unknown in Europe at that time.
3. True
4. True
5. False. Though pigs' feet were eaten, they were never candied.
6. True
7. True
8. True
9. False. Though he enjoyed food, he never imported Middle Eastern chefs.
10. True

MULTIPLE CHOICE

1. B
2. D
3. A
4. B
5. C

Spice It Up

TRUE OR FALSE

1. False. There are almost as many varieties of curry in India as there are people making it.
2. True
3. True
4. True
5. False. Saffron was greatly enjoyed in Rome and was frequently used as a symbol of good fortune and prosperity.
6. False. Though some spices will help keep pests away, it's not enough to truly preserve meat - salting was the preservation of choice.
7. True
8. True
9. False. Many remedies were suggested, but it seems that either a small procedure to correct phimosis or a talk with his brother-in-law, Emperor Joseph, did the trick.

10. False. They were buried with many things, but not garlic.

MULTIPLE CHOICE

1. B
2. A
3. D
4. C
5. A

Unusual Foods

TRUE OR FALSE

1. True
2. True
3. False. Though alligator can be tasty, it is not part of a state dish.
4. False. A cockentrice is actually the top half of a chicken sewn to the bottom half of a pig.
5. True
6. True
7. True
8. False. Beaver was never considered a vegetable. It was, however, considered to be a fish at one point, and so acceptable for Lent.
9. True
10. True

MULTIPLE CHOICE

1. A
2. C
3. B
4. D
5. A

Table Manners

TRUE OR FALSE

1. True
2. True
3. False. Some cultures *do* find this an acceptable way of complimenting the food, but it is not polite at all in South Korea.
4. True
5. False. Tablecloths were for decoration and not for staining with food, particularly as they could be quite expensive.

6. False. Queen Victoria was a notoriously fast eater, meaning that she finished way before the other guests. Since she was queen, the meal was officially over when she was done, leaving many guests still hungry.
7. True
8. True
9. False. Knives were the one piece of tableware that guests were expected to bring on their own.
10. False. There were many shortages, but cutlery was not one of them.

MULTIPLE CHOICE

1. B
2. C
3. D
4. A
5. B

Fast Food

TRUE OR FALSE

1. False. Fries have always been a popular side owing to the cheapness of potatoes.
2. True
3. True
4. False. The name comes from the founder Glen Bell and his original business of selling tacos.
5. False. Saloons did not have ride-thru service. In fact, some towns had laws against riding a horse while drunk.
6. True
7. False. Oysters were a very common food for the poor because they were so cheap and easy to collect.
8. True
9. False. Colonel Sanders, the founder of KFC, was from Kentucky.
10. True

MULTIPLE CHOICE

1. B
2. B
3. A
4. D
5. C

CHAPTER 3:
WAR AND CONFLICT

THE FRENCH REVOLUTION

TRUE OR FALSE

1. Marie Antoinette famously said, "Let them eat cake!" because eggs were cheaper than flour and could be used to make cake batter.
2. The Revolutionaries introduced a new calendar system, called the French Republican Calendar, that was meant to erase all religious and royalist holidays.
3. Though the monarchy was abolished in September 1792, it was not until January 1793 that King Louis XVI was executed.
4. The Revolution was well-received across all of France.
5. Maximilian Robespierre proposed a new religion for France after the Revolution, called the Cult of the Supreme Being.
6. Red cravats and neckcloths came into fashion as a way to show support for the revolutionaries and the justice they meted out with the guillotine.
7. From June 1793 to July 1794, during a year known as the Reign of Terror, about 16,000 people were executed to preserve the newly formed republic.
8. Jean-Paul Marat was stabbed to death by Charlotte Corday while in his bathtub.
9. Following the adoption of a constitution in 1793, French women enjoyed full citizenship.
10. Marie Antoinette had a secret, illicit affair with King Louis XVI's sister, which led to them not consummating their marriage for many years and turned the public against her.

MULTIPLE CHOICE

1. At the time of the French Revolution, the average French citizen ate how much bread per day?

A. Two ounces
B. One pound
C. Five kilos
D. Two pounds

2. The guillotine, which saw much use during the Revolution, and later during the Reign of Terror, was also known as:

A. Madame Efficiency
B. The Problem Solver
C. The National Razor
D. The King un-Maker

3. When angry French citizens took to the streets of Paris, they dismantled what by hand, and later sold or gave away the bricks?

A. Palace of Justice
B. The Bastille
C. The Louvre Palace
D. Versailles

4. King Louis XVI and Marie Antoinette attempted to flee France in disguise, but were apprehended in Varennes when:

A. Marie Antoinette gave silver dishes to a helpful local official
B. Servants still observed protocol regarding eminence to the King and Queen, though they were supposed to be disguised as peasants
C. Louis XVI was recognized from his image on money
D. All of the above

5. The frequently pornographic and satirical pamphlets about the French king and queen, as well as the royal court, were known as:

A. *Libelles*
B. *Petits mensonges*
C. *Tristes vérités*
D. *Calomnies*

THE BRITISH EMPIRE

TRUE OR FALSE

1. During the American Revolution, Paul Revere made the longest ride through the Colonies to warn the militia that the British were coming.
2. The Great Game was a rivalry between the 19th-century British and Russian Empires over influence in Central Asia, primarily in Afghanistan, Persia, and Tibet.
3. The Boer Wars were fought between Britain and the originally Dutch colonists in South Africa for control of the area after Britain bought the colony from the Dutch government.
4. The East India Company relied on the British military to guard its interests.
5. Britain became the dominant naval power in the world after the defeat of the French Armada in 1592.
6. The Berlin Conference between 1884 and 1885 established an orderly process of European colonial expansion in what came to be known as the "Scramble for Africa."
7. Queen Victoria was the only British monarch to adopt the moniker of "Empress/Emperor of India."
8. Cecil Rhodes and his British South Africa company were the driving force behind the building of a railroad from Cairo in the north to Cape Town in the south.
9. Near the end of the 19th century, a genre of literature emerged called *belle epoque* that centered on fears of a dwindling British Empire.
10. *The Durham Report* from 1839 proposed unification and self-governance of the upper and lower Canadian colonies as a solution to the general political unrest and the armed riots of 1837.

MULTIPLE CHOICE

1. During the American Revolution, roughly what proportion of the Continental Army was Black?

A. 5%
B. 3%
C. 1%
D. None

2. To put the lucrative cotton industry under British control, the East India Company or soldiers of the British Raj would:

A. Break the weaver's hands so that they couldn't work for long stretches of time
B. Cut off two or more fingers of weavers and spinners so that they couldn't ply their trade anymore
C. Smash looms and spinning wheels so that they couldn't compete with British factories
D. All of the above

3. Hitler cited many things as inspirations for his ideology. These included:

A. The treatment of prisoners and Indigenous people in the Boer War
B. The British Empire's subjugation of colonies, particularly India
C. Neither A nor B
D. Both A and B

4. From 1938–1942, Britain attempted to invade:

A. Turkey
B. Nepal
C. Afghanistan
D. Finland

5. The origins of which war are still debated and not entirely understood from the modern perspective, but the United States' desire to expand into Canada is seen as a possible motive?

A. War of 1812
B. French and Indian War
C. War of Spanish Succession
D. King Philip's War

WORLD WAR I

TRUE OR FALSE

1. The moving of large numbers of soldiers and civilian refugees during World War I was a major contributor to the spread of the Spanish Flu.
2. Zebras were called into service to support the Allied efforts in Africa due to a shortage of horses.
3. Unlike World War II, there was no rationing of food during WWI because so many nations were still self-reliant in that regard.
4. The extension of the war in Europe to the various colonial holdings of the involved nations caused Japan to declare war on Germany before invading and seizing control of the German holdings in the Pacific Ocean.
5. The assassination of Archduke Franz Ferdinand and his wife was the only reason that WWI broke out.
6. Though airplanes had been invented, zeppelins were far more important to the war.
7. Support from colonial holdings was very important during World War I, and no less than 140,000 soldiers from India served under British command on the Western Front between 1914 and 1918.
8. Though women on both sides assisted with the war effort, it had little effect on the push for women's suffrage in Britain and the United States.
9. When the pre-war use of massed infantry proved to be obsolete in the face of machine gun emplacements and advanced artillery, the armies of Europe turned to chemical weapons to even the odds.
10. Many animals were called up to help with the war effort, including at least one elephant in Britain.

MULTIPLE CHOICE

1. During WWI, Americans were so distrustful of anything German that:

A. German shepherd dogs were sometimes killed
B. Frankfurters were called "liberty sausages"
C. Sauerkraut was called "liberty cabbage"
D. All of the above

2. Because of the combination of terrible injuries and advances in medical science, 1917 saw the establishment of the first:

A. Dedicated field hospital tent
B. Blood bank
C. Amputations under anesthesia
D. Mobile medical vehicles

3. To avoid writing to his children about the horrors of the war while in the trenches, who created the *Dr. Dolittle* stories?

A. C. S. Lewis
B. Rudyard Kipling
C. Hugh Laurie
D. Hugh Lofting

4. Despite being supplied with a daily ration of rum with their kit, British soldiers were *not* initially equipped with:

A. Helmets
B. Boots
C. Bayonets
D. Trench knives

5. One of the major contributors to Germany's defeat in WWI was the shortages brought on by the Blockade of Germany - and most notably, a lack of what?

A. Bread
B. Horses
C. Gasoline
D. Medical supplies

WORLD WAR II

TRUE OR FALSE

1. Upon hearing stories of the horrors Jews faced in Europe, the United States welcomed all Jewish refugees.
2. At the end of the war, German food rationing was so severe that the population resorted to making bread from grass and silage.
3. The Ukrainian born Soviet sniper Lyudmila Mikhailovna Pavlichenko had over 300 confirmed kills and was a close personal friend of First Lady Eleanor Roosevelt.
4. Hitler's 1939 invasion of Poland was the first expansion Germany attempted in the prelude to WWII.
5. Japan attacked Pearl Harbor in 1941, but Germany did not declare war on the United States in support of their Axis ally until 1943.
6. After the war, as the victors divided the national territories between themselves and established the new borders, Germany lost a quarter of its pre-war territory.
7. Benito Mussolini saw himself as a defender of the Catholic faith, which he believed to be the traditional right of all Italians.
8. The Japanese marine engineer Tsutomu Yamaguchi is the only person to be officially recognized by the Japanese government as a survivor of the nuclear bombing of *both* Hiroshima and Nagasaki.
9. The French Resistance was reluctant use celebrities and other easily recognized people.
10. Both Germany and the Soviet Union had no desire to get involved in the Spanish Civil War, citing a policy of stringent isolationism.

MULTIPLE CHOICE

1. The last Japanese soldier from WWII to surrender finally did so in:

A. 1952
B. 1974
C. 1949
D. 1962

2. During pilot training, how many pilots died?

A. 15,000
B. 12,000
C. 2,000
D. 17,000

3. The United States experimented with the idea of loading bombs with what animals, which were then fitted with smaller bombs they could distribute through cities?

A. Pigeons
B. Cats
C. Bats
D. Rats

4. Though it was never implemented, the British developed a plan known as "Operation Vegetarian," in which Germany's livestock would be targeted through:

A. Targeted bombing raids
B. Dropping anthrax-laced linseed cakes for animals to find
C. Infecting animals with contagious diseases and then turning them loose in Germany
D. All of the above

5. Once the Allies were defeated, Hitler planned on attacking which country next?

A. Switzerland
B. Italy
C. China
D. Spain

THE COLD WAR

TRUE OR FALSE

1. The term "third-world country" refers to the economic and cultural development of a nation.
2. Though the Cold War remained officially cold between the Eastern and Western powers, it was quite hot in a number of local proxy wars where combatants were supported by both sides.
3. Following World War II, Germany was divided neatly down the middle by the Western Allies and the Soviet Union.
4. The term "Cold War" was first used by author George Orwell in his essay "You and the Atomic Bomb," published in the *Tribune* in 1945.
5. Despite a lot of blustering, at no point during the Cuban Missile Crisis was there actually any real danger of a nuclear exchange.
6. A policy of détente, aiming to reduce tension and hostilities, collapsed at the beginning of the 1980s, when US President Ronald Reagan started increasing economic, diplomatic, and military pressure on the Soviet Union.
7. The United States policy of opposing Communism worldwide was known as the "Roosevelt Doctrine" in memory of President Roosevelt.
8. Ho Chi Minh and the Viet Minh never received aid from the United States in their quest for independence.
9. Though the Iron Curtain began as a political metaphor describing the division between East and West, it eventually came to refer to the 4,350-mile-long physical barrier separating the Soviet Union from the rest of Europe.
10. Before the Korean War, the Korean Peninsula had been solely ruled over by China.

MULTIPLE CHOICE

1. During the Cold War, in cooperation with a local organization, America sent 20,000 'what' to Romania, which were diverted to a paper recycling mill and turned into toilet paper?

A. Dictionaries with the word "dictator" highlighted
B. Bibles
C. Copies of *Animal Farm*
D. Issues of *Life* magazine

2. Which famous "nuclear film" featured such detailed shots of the interior of a B-52 bomber that the director was afraid he was going to get reported to the FBI for trying to smuggle secrets to the Russians?

A. *Plan 9 From Outer Space*
B. *Failsafe*
C. *War Games*
D. *Dr. Strangelove*

3. In the 1960s, there was a plan to humiliate Fidel Castro in front of the Cuban public by:

A. Using thallium salts, a depilatory, to make his beard fall out
B. Stealing his pants from the hotel laundry and hemming them to make them appear too short
C. Putting a dye on his cigars so that it would appear he was wearing lipstick
D. Hiding bleaching agents in his hat so that he would appear to be going prematurely gray

4. During the development of a new type of ejector seat for bombers capable of traveling faster than the speed of sound, the United States Air Force used what to test the new seats?

A. Crash test dummies invented in 1949
B. Cadavers
C. Drugged bears
D. An early form of ballistics gel with pig bones suspended within

5. Operation Chrome Dome, which ran from 1961–1968, was a plan by the United States to:

A. Begin installing lead-lined roofs into government buildings to mitigate the damage from nuclear fallout
B. Ensure that at least one bomber carrying a payload of nuclear bombs was kept in the air at all times
C. Build an "apocalypse-proof" shelter into the mountains of Virginia for government officials
D. Spray Soviet collective farms with a chromium-based powder, ensuring that the people who ate them would develop long-term health problems

ANSWER KEYS:

The French Revolution

TRUE OR FALSE

1. False. She never said, "Let them eat cake," or any variation thereof. It was pure propaganda, with the phrase originating before she was even made queen.
2. True
3. True
4. False. France devolved into civil war with great casualties on both sides.
5. True
6. False. The "Red Cap of Liberty" was the accessory of choice to show one's allegiance with the revolutionaries.
7. True
8. True
9. False. Though women had played an integral role in the Revolution, they were denied citizenship.
10. False. Their marriage remained unconsummated for a variety of reasons, but any notion of a sapphic affair is purely the work of the anti-monarchists who wanted to discredit Marie Antoinette.

MULTIPLE CHOICE

1. D
2. C
3. B
4. D
5. A

The British Empire

TRUE OR FALSE

1. False. Sybil Ludington, a teenage girl, rode farther while also avoiding capture.
2. True
3. True
4. False. The East India Company became notorious for its paramilitary forces.
5. False. It was the Spanish Armada that was defeated in 1588.
6. True
7. False. She was the first, but others assumed the title until India gained independence.
8. True
9. False. It was called *fin de siècle*, or "end of an age."
10. True

MULTIPLE CHOICE

1. A
2. D
3. D
4. C
5. A

World War I

TRUE OR FALSE

1. True
2. False. Zebras have never been used as anything more than a curiosity, as they are not domesticated at all.
3. False. WWI saw great rationing, even after the war was over.
4. True
5. False. The assassination was merely the final nail in the coffin. Europe was a powder keg of various alliances, with an arms race buildup between Great Britain and Russia.
6. False. Fixed-wing aircraft were extremely important to intel gathering and early aerial combat.
7. True
8. False. Their efforts during the war were frequently cited as proof that they were worthy of the right to vote.
9. True
10. True

MULTIPLE CHOICE

1. D
2. B
3. D
4. A
5. B

World War II

TRUE OR FALSE

1. False. The United States turned away many ships with refugees fleeing Germany. Many others had their applications for American visas denied before even making it onto a ship, including Anne Frank and her family.
2. True
3. True
4. False. Germany had already expanded into other countries, including Austria and Yugoslavia. The rest of Europe hoped that this would appease Hitler's ambition, and that he would stop there.
5. False. Germany preemptively declared war on the United States immediately following Pearl Harbor.
6. True
7. False. Mussolini was critical of the Catholic Church and organized religion as a whole.
8. True
9. False. The French Resistance used many celebrities, including Josephine Baker, believing that their fame would prevent them from being suspected of spying.
10. False. Both Germany and the Soviet Union used the Spanish Civil War as a way to test new arms and tactics.

MULTIPLE CHOICE

1. B
2. A
3. C
4. B
5. A

The Cold War

TRUE OR FALSE

1. False. This term simply refers to nations that remained neutral in the Cold War, not joining NATO or the Soviet Union's allies.
2. True
3. False. The division of Germany was a messy affair, with the city of Berlin - deep in East Germany - being itself divided.
4. True
5. False. A Soviet nuclear submarine was prepared to launch missiles, believing they were under fire when an American sub that was attempting to map the area dropped depth charges to detect underwater rock formations. The American didn't realize a Soviet sub was in the area as well.
6. True
7. False. It was known as the "Truman Doctrine."
8. False. The United States happily provided aid, wishing to promote the idea of democracy. Aid was quickly withdrawn when the French gained the upper hand again.
9. True
10. False. Japan had long ruled over Korea.

MULTIPLE CHOICE

1. B
2. D
3. A
4. C
5. B

CHAPTER 4:
ART

GREEK/ROMAN ART

TRUE OR FALSE

1. Roman painting depicts themes of a wide variety, ranging from mythology and portraits to still life and everyday imagery.
2. Ancient Greece was largely unified, which can make it difficult to place the origins of some pieces.
3. While greatly influenced by Greek and Etruscan sculpture, the native Roman style can be found predominantly in the tombs of the wealthy where busts of the deceased were placed.
4. It was considered taboo to paint scenes of war or violence on temples in Rome.
5. During Roman conquest, they would erase all images of local gods and goddesses, replacing them with Roman ones and forbidding the old religion.
6. While many art pieces depict mythology and everyday life, there were exceptions. In the city of Pompeii, stone penises can be found skillfully carved into walls all over the city.
7. Greek and Roman marble sculptures were left unpainted to showcase the purity of the stone and the artistic achievement of the sculptor.
8. Glass was used to create luxury art for the enjoyment of wealthy Romans, and came in a large variety of styles, colors, and techniques.
9. Thanks to the abundance and durability of coins, we have a vast sample of Greek aesthetics beyond statues and pottery.
10. The famous Elgin Marbles were removed to Britain with the blessing of the Greek government in the hopes that they would be kept safe during war with the Ottoman Empire.

MULTIPLE CHOICE

1. Though they paid homage to the Greeks, ancient Roman art differed in that they also explored:

A. Pottery paintings
B. Diorama sculpture
C. Landscapes
D. Illuminated manuscripts

2. The main colors on classical Greek pottery or terracottas are:

A. Blue and green
B. Red and black
C. Brown and white
D. Yellow and black

3. Greek silver objects, such as ornate drinking vessels, were once worth more than gold. They were stamped with a maker's mark and:

A. The weight of the object because it was likely to be smelted at some point
B. A dedication to a specific god so that it would confer blessings on the owner
C. The owner's name to curtail thieving
D. The place it was made, as local identity and pride was of great significance

4. Fayum mummy portraits were common in Roman-ruled Egypt, and were:

A. Portraits carved into sandstone of Egyptian sarcophagus
B. Paintings on the insides of tombs of family members of the deceased
C. Painted portraits on wooden panels that were affixed to the mummies of the upper class
D. Small figurines meant to represent the deceased and ensure their safe passage to the afterlife

5. An essential mainstay in the homes of the rich was which decoration, which could be seen on small statues, furniture, and jewelry?

A. Metalwork
B. Woodcarving
C. Glassware
D. Porcelain

THE RENAISSANCE

TRUE OR FALSE

1. The Renaissance erupted as a spontaneous expression of artistic innovation.
2. The statue that launched Michelangelo to fame as a sculptor was a fake - it was a copy he made of an actual Roman statue of the god Eros.
3. Donato di Niccolò di Betto Bardi, known mostly as Donatello, was the first Renaissance sculptor to create a freestanding nude statue since the fall of the Roman empire. It depicted biblical hero David.
4. Sponsoring art was an important act of displaying wealth and influence, and the powerful Medici family were patrons of famous artists like Donatello, Michelangelo, Raphael, and Leonardo.
5. Art of the 15th–17th centuries was exclusively religious due to the power of the Catholic Church and exempt from influence by Humanist philosophies.
6. Michelangelo was unpopular in his lifetime, dying impoverished and in relative obscurity.
7. The Renaissance began in Italy in the early 1400s, but it would be over a hundred years before the art, along with Renaissance science and philosophy, would reach Scotland.
8. Painting and sculpture were more influenced by myth and legend than concepts such as proportion and mathematics.
9. While most artists of the Tudor court were imported foreigners, Britain had a strong native artistic style of painted miniature portraits.
10. Napoleon Bonaparte famously hated the Mona Lisa, as it reminded him of his youth in Italy.

MULTIPLE CHOICE

1. Of the following, who is *not* considered a Renaissance artist?

A. Hans Holbein
B. Hieronymus Bosch
C. El Greco
D. Marco Cardisco

2. Renaissance architecture focused on proportions, geometry, and what?

A. Irregularity
B. Innovation
C. Symmetry
D. Austereness

3. The Dutch and Flemish painters took inspiration from Italian art, but developed their own style, which lacked the lightness of the Italian style but expressed their interest in:

A. Nature
B. The ocean
C. Cityscapes
D. Portraiture

4. Renaissance-style art began to show up in Germany in which century?

A. 14th
B. 16th
C. 17th
D. 15th

5. The painting of what marks the end of the early Renaissance in Italy?

A. The Last Supper
B. Sistine Chapel
C. Equestrian Portrait of Charles V
D. The Ambassadors

BAROQUE, ROCOCO, AND ROMANTICISM

TRUE OR FALSE

1. The Baroque aesthetic was a direct rejection of the austerity the Catholic Church imposed in the 16th century.
2. The first baroque influences in the Hispanic Americas were from Sevillan Tenebrism, which focuses on dark backgrounds and contrast with bright colors.
3. In the rococo painting "The Swing," a young woman on a swing, pushed by her much older husband, provides a scandalous yet playful upskirt look to a young man hiding in some bushes.
4. The painter Caravaggio was known for his piety and humble way of living.
5. "Baroque" was an entirely flattering term used to describe the richness of the art.
6. The spirit of Rococo began to be attacked in the mid-18th century, after the rise of Enlightenment criticism and the puritanical ideals of the middle class.
7. Rococo art is far more concerned with mythological and religious figures than ordinary people.
8. Many Rococo painters rejected pastoral scenes and the Romantic idea of a shepherd because they were too chaotic and did not fit within the carefully structured art.
9. In the visual arts, Romanticism first showed itself in landscape painting, where British artists in the 1760s began to paint wild landscapes and storms, in addition to Gothic architecture.
10. *The Raft of the Medusa* is a purely allegorical painting, with the sailors' suffering meant to represent the fall of Man without salvation.

MULTIPLE CHOICE

1. William Blake was one of several Romantic artists whose art could be described as:

A. Demure
B. Pious
C. Realistic
D. Mystical

2. The spiritual element of Rococo was popular in central Europe, Portugal, and which other country?

A. Russia
B. South America
C. Spain
D. Greece

3. Romantic era architecture was inspired by the which style?

A. Gothic
B. Egyptian
C. Minimalist
D. Byzantine

4. The first use of the word Rococo in print in 1825 was to describe decoration that was:

A. Daring
B. Innovative
C. Old fashioned
D. Traditional

5. Baroque sculpture was elaborate and featured multiple what?

A. People per sculpture
B. Ideal viewing angles
C. Symbolic designs
D. Layers

THE SURREALISTS

TRUE OR FALSE

1. Though bronze casting was outlawed during Germany's occupation of Paris, Picasso continued to do it with bronze smuggled to him by the French Resistance.
2. The centaur was a famous symbol adopted by the Surrealists and appeared in many of their works.
3. While works of Surrealism feature the element of surprise, unexpected combination of elements, and *non sequitur*, many Surrealist artists consider their work a philosophical expression much more than they think of it as art.
4. Frida Kahlo was notoriously private and had no desire for recognition in her own lifetime.
5. Politically, the Surrealist art movement was Communistic and Anarchistic.
6. Surrealist art commonly depicts illogical or dreamlike scenes with the intention of allowing the unconscious mind to express itself.
7. Walt Disney rejected a proposal to create an animated feature with Salvador Dali outright.
8. Meret Elisabeth Oppenheim was a Surrealist artist who experimented with X-ray art, using everyday objects to represent female sexuality and the exploitation of this sexuality.
9. The Surrealists believed that the only way to find the truth in an object was to observe it in its normal, mundane surroundings.
10. Food and eating were extremely important to Salvador Dalí's artistic work. He associated food with sex and was obsessed with the fact that the female praying mantis eats the male after mating with him.

MULTIPLE CHOICE

1. Besides her many self-portraits, Frida Kahlo was inspired by Mexican nature and what?

A. Art deco
B. Its historical artifacts
C. The ocean
D. The Catholic Church

2. In the years just before and during World War II, to escape fascist and Nazi persecution, to where did many Surrealist artists flee?

A. New York
B. Moscow
C. London
D. Cairo

3. When was the golden age of Surrealism?

A. 1930s
B. 1920s
C. 1940s
D. All of the above

4. Due to the strangeness of his paintings, which artist is sometimes mentioned as a possible precursor artist for Surrealism?

A. Hieronymus Bosch
B. Giuseppe Arcimboldo
C. Joos de Momper
D. All of the above

5. Which Surrealist artist is seen as an important figure for feminist identification?

A. Jaine Larsson
B. Micaela von Darel
C. Meret Elisabeth Oppenheim
D. Roberta Tailor

MODERN ART

TRUE OR FALSE

1. Jackson Pollock developed his style completely spontaneously.
2. The term "Modern Art" is normally applied to art where the spirit of experimentation takes center stage, pushing the traditional methods to the side, and creating art with much more abstract content.
3. The painting "The Luncheon on the Grass" was originally rejected from the art salons not because of the nudity, but because the naked woman was looking directly at the viewer, making them be there for her, rather than the other way around.
4. The vibrant colors in the sky of Edward Munch's *The Scream* are due to the effects of a volcanic eruption.
5. After World War II, the United States became a focal point for modern art and saw well over a dozen new art genres emerging.
6. Modern contemporary genre art is meant to be easy to understand, focusing on simple forms and colors instead of deeper meanings.
7. Performance or action art originated in the 1960s as part of the Counterculture movement.
8. Of the approximately 2,100 artworks by Vincent van Gogh, including around 860 oil paintings, most were created in the last two years of his life.
9. In Conceptual art, the concepts or ideas involved in the work have greater priority than the traditional aesthetic, materials, and methods of the art.
10. Andy Warhol worked exclusively with silkscreen printing.

MULTIPLE CHOICE

1. The era of Modern Art stretches from which decade to the 1970s?

A. 1950s
B. 1930s
C. 1910s
D. 1860s

2. Henri Matisse's painting *Dance (I)*, featuring five naked dancing women, was much liked by its creator, who described it as:

A. "The essence of nude freedom"
B. "The joy of womanhood"
C. "The overpowering climax of luminosity"
D. "The true nature of moral corruption"

3. *Fountain* is an artwork from 1917 made simply from what?

A. A urinal laid on its back
B. A watering can
C. An early dildo
D. A mess of water pipes

4. What is the art period following Modern Art called?

A. Avant-garde
B. Postmodernism
C. Impressionism
D. Cubist analysis

5. By the end of the 1970s, many art critics had started talking about what in reference to the current status of the modern art scene?

A. The life support of art
B. The beginning of true innovation
C. The end of painting
D. The suffering of aesthetics

ANSWER KEYS:

Greek/Roman Art

TRUE OR FALSE

1. True
2. False. Ancient Greece was more of a collection of loosely affiliated city-states than a true country, with many having their own unique styles.
3. True
4. False. The Romans loved a good war scene.
5. False. The Romans largely left the local religion and customs in place, so long as the Roman Pantheon was also used. This led to many local religions fusing with the Roman.
6. True
7. False. Sculptures were brightly painted.
8. True
9. True
10. False. The Earl of Elgin was only supposed to be cataloging them and taking casts where appropriate. He made the decision to remove them wholesale on his own initiative.

MULTIPLE CHOICE

1. C
2. B
3. A
4. C
5. A

The Renaissance

TRUE OR FALSE

1. False. The Renaissance was the product of scholarly advancements and contact with the Middle East.
2. True
3. True
4. True
5. False. Art began to become more secular, with many artists painting scenes from mythology and real life.
6. False. Michelangelo was immensely popular and had great wealth when he died, though he chose to live simply.
7. True
8. False. Ideas on proportion, ratio, and perspective play an important part in Renaissance art.
9. True
10. False. He liked the painting so much that he had it placed in his bedroom while he was emperor.

MULTIPLE CHOICE

1. B
2. C
3. A
4. D
5. B

Baroque, Rococo, and Romanticism

TRUE OR FALSE

1. False. In response to the spartan look of the Reformation, the Catholic Church became more ornate than ever, and Baroque was the result.
2. True
3. True
4. False. Caravaggio was a well-known troublemaker, carrying on affairs and drinking heavily throughout his life, as well as being involved in at least one murder.
5. False. Baroque was originally a derisive term, with the aesthetic being widely mocked.
6. True
7. False. Many artists began to celebrate the ordinary and mundane as truly Romantic and heroic. Shepherds, laborers, and everyday pastoral scenes took center stage.
8. False. Shepherd boys in particular were a common motif.
9. True
10. False. The *Medusa* was a real ship that was famously wrecked. The ordeal of the survivors was well-documented and closely followed through newspapers.

MULTIPLE CHOICE

1. D
2. B
3. A
4. C
5. B

The Surrealists

TRUE OR FALSE

1. True
2. False. It was the minotaur that the Surrealists adopted.
3. True
4. False. Frida Kahlo very much wanted to be known as a painter in her own right and had several solo exhibitions in her lifetime.
5. True
6. True
7. False. Walt Disney and Salvador Dali were eager to collaborate, though their project was only finished in 2003, after both were dead.
8. True
9. False. One of the major principles of Surrealism was to take ordinary objects out of their context and to attempt to find meaning in them.
10. True

MULTIPLE CHOICE

1. B
2. A
3. A
4. D
5. C

Modern Art

TRUE OR FALSE

1. False. Pollock observed other artists working in a similar manner and adopted the approach for himself.
2. True
3. True
4. False. It's unclear what caused such a vibrant sky that inspired Munch; most likely it was a natural phenomenon that happens far north.
5. True
6. False. Modern art is meant to challenge the viewer, without clear meaning.
7. False. Action art originated far earlier than that in the early 20th century, possibly as far back as the 1800s.
8. True
9. True
10. False. Warhol worked with a variety of mediums, including traditional paint and brushes.

MULTIPLE CHOICE

1. D
2. C
3. A
4. B
5. C

CHAPTER 5: ENTERTAINMENT

MUSIC

TRUE OR FALSE

1. Despite the early start to his career, Mozart composed few completed works during his lifetime.
2. Pete Best and Paul McCartney were deported from Germany in the early stage of their career because they set fire to a condom in a hallway and were arrested for arson.
3. Percussionists as early as the 1860s began combining drums and cymbals, which would eventually become the modern drum kit.
4. Beethoven learned to play the piano by cutting the legs off it so that he could feel the vibrations through the floor.
5. Contrary to the popular myth, music tempo actually has no effect on human heart rates.
6. The recording company EMI used some of its extraordinary profits to help develop the CT scan.
7. Neanderthals had no concept of music and made no musical instruments of their own.
8. Following the Jacobite uprising, bagpipes were banned in Scotland in 1745 as instruments of war.
9. In France in 1518, a strange phenomenon of "dancing plague" broke out where up to 400 people danced for weeks on end.
10. Napoleon once owned a famed Stradivarius violin.

MULTIPLE CHOICE

1. The three most famous bands of the beginning of the Heavy Metal genre are Deep Purple, Led Zeppelin, and which other band?

A. Kiss
B. Black Sabbath
C. Alice Cooper
D. Iron Maiden

2. To which of these groups was music considered sacred and a necessity for a functional society?

A. Aborigines
B. Olmec
C. Gauls
D. Sumerians

3. What is the oldest known musical instrument, dating from over 40,000 years ago?

A. Bone flute
B. Drum
C. Wood xylophone
D. Bone wind chimes

4. Musical therapy is used particularly commonly used with:

A. Adolescents
B. The elderly
C. Dogs with anxiety
D. B and C

5. What is the scientific study of music called?

A. Audiology
B. Orbology
C. Ethnology
D. Musicology

TELEVISION

TRUE OR FALSE

1. Despite popular belief, the 1968 *Star Trek* episode "Plato's Stepchildren" is not the first television show to depict an interracial kiss.
2. *The Munsters* was the first show to depict a husband and wife sharing one bed instead of sleeping in separate beds.
3. The first televised sporting event was a baseball game in 1939 between Columbia and Princeton.
4. Executives forbade Lucille Ball from performing her own stunts, afraid that she might injure herself and have to take time off from filming *I Love Lucy.*
5. The *Futurama Theorem* is a real-life math formula created just for an episode of the show to solve a body swap problem.
6. The Nickelodeon cartoon *Hey Arnold!* is credited with saving at least two lives after an episode showing how to perform the Heimlich maneuver aired.
7. The first television station was established in 1937, mainly as a means of broadcasting news regarding the tense situation in Europe.
8. Color TV wasn't considered viable, or even desirable, until the 1960s because of concern about viewers' ocular nerves.
9. To avoid confusion between the shows *The Addams Family* and *The Munsters,* they went to great lengths to avoid hiring the same guest stars.
10. The number of people that tuned in to watch the verdict in the OJ Simpson murder trial surpassed that of the viewers of the Apollo 11 moon landing.

MULTIPLE CHOICE

1. Derived from the use of cathode-ray vacuum glass tubes inside the TV itself, what is a UK slang term for a TV?

A. The Vac
B. The Cat
C. The Glass
D. The Tube

2. In what year did the radio show *Texaco Star Theatre* make the move to television to become the first regular TV show?

A. 1932
B. 1941
C. 1948
D. 1950

3. The first 3D television prototype was demonstrated in what year?

A. 1928
B. 1946
C. 1984
D. 2003

4. Wireless TV signals sent from a ground-based transmitter, as opposed to a satellite, are called what?

A. Terrestrial television
B. Hydrospheric television
C. Over-the-air television
D. A and C

5. The first experimental TV systems were mechanical, and used what to produce the picture?

A. A neon light and a spinning disk
B. A series of tiny lamps and a water pump
C. A large lamp shining through thin moving metal plates overlaid on each other
D. A rotating cylinder projector

MOVIES

TRUE OR FALSE

1. The first movie about the sinking of the Titanic wasn't made until the 1940s, as it was considered far too sensitive of a subject.
2. Walt Disney developed surround sound for its film *Fantasia.*
3. Hitler and the Nazi party were great fans of the 1930 film *All Quiet on the Western Front* because it depicted German soldiers sympathetically.
4. The famous scene in *Frankenstein* (1931) where the assistant drops the brain in the jar, and it is replaced with an "abnormal" brain is based on the destruction of Walt Whitman's brain in the same manner after he had donated it for study.
5. President Woodrow Wilson was disgusted by D. W. Griffith's infamous *The Birth of a Nation* and refused to screen it in the White House.
6. Contrary to popular belief, George Lucas did not discover Harrison Ford while he was working as a carpenter on a movie set.
7. While miniatures are a common special effect device, the tyrannosaurus-rex in *Jurassic Park* was life-sized and weighed as much as a real tyrannosaurus.
8. The first science fiction movie was produced in 1941.
9. The cat that Marlon Brando holds in *The Godfather* was actually his cat that he spontaneously brought to set.
10. During the filming of the chest burster scene in *Alien*, the crew had been informed about the creature emerging from the chest of its host but not that fake blood would be spraying all over the set. This led to their reactions being their natural out-of-character response to what they thought was a real injury.

MULTIPLE CHOICE

1. When the first movies that were not silent came to the cinemas, what were they commonly called?

A. Audibles
B. Sounders
C. Talkies
D. Flashies

2. The first Academy Awards were held in what year?

A. 1899
B. 1917
C. 1929
D. 1936

3. The first patent for a 3D film-making process was filed in what year?

A. 1890
B. 1946
C. 1979
D. 2003

4. Underwater motion capture was first used in the creation of which movie?

A. *The Matrix: Reloaded*
B. *Star Wars Episode One: The Phantom Menace*
C. *Waterworld*
D. *Avatar: The Way of Water*

5. Which was the first film to use Technicolor?

A. *The Wizard of Oz*
B. *The Gulf Between*
C. *Wings*
D. *Frankenstein*

THEATRE

TRUE OR FALSE

1. The longest-running play in history is *The Mousetrap* by Agatha Christie, which has run since 1952 (barring a short break during the COVID-19 pandemic in 2020).
2. The Globe Theatre was the first purpose-built theater in Britain.
3. "Off-Broadway" refers to any play that is first performed in New York's theater district but not actually on the street Broadway.
4. Disney parks are actually considered large-scale theaters.
5. Contrary to popular belief, Shakespeare's *Macbeth* isn't the unluckiest of his plays. In fact, more actors have died during stagings of *Hamlet*.
6. Pyrotechnics weren't adopted as special effects in theaters until the 1700s when gunpowder lowered in price.
7. It's considered bad luck to acknowledge ghosts that may be haunting a theater.
8. Paul Kieve, a British illusionist, holds the world record for most costume changes at 29 in a single show.
9. *Cats* is the longest-running musical in history.
10. Bram Stoker once worked as an actor in Dublin.

MULTIPLE CHOICE

1. Where did arguably the first theater performances take place in ancient Greece, with mandatory attendance?

A. Auditoriums
B. Palladiums
C. Dionysia
D. Heretia

2. In China, stage actors are commonly known as what, in honor of the first acting school established in the 8th century BCE?

A. Children of the Pear Garden
B. Shadows on the Silk Breeze
C. Masked Heroes of the First Water
D. Citizens of the Orchard

3. The Latin term *deus ex machina* refers to mechanical devices used to bring an actor portraying a deity onto the stage, usually to resolve a dramatic situation or conclude a storyline. The term originated in which theater?

A. Renaissance
B. Roman
C. Early Spanish
D. Ancient Greek

4. Most of the earliest modern examples of true musicals were actually quite bawdy and not appropriate for children. They usually took what form?

A. Minstrel shows
B. Ballad-farces
C. Operettas
D. *Comédie en vaudeville*

5. Much of early modern theater relied on stock characters. Which two stock characters are commonly featured in comedies?

A. Harlequin and Pantalone
B. Sadness and Mirth
C. Stocking and Hat
D. Art and Logic

GAMES

TRUE OR FALSE

1. Board games date back to the 16th century, when they were part of educating young men and boys on strategy.
2. *Mortal Kombat* was the first video game to depict blood and gore.
3. Nintendo, famous for its home video game systems, was founded in 1889 and produced playing cards.
4. The 1975 arcade game *Gun Fight* was the first of its kind to use a microprocessor.
5. *Pong* was the first video game to be invented.
6. The first game to be played over a network of computers was *Snipes* in 1983.
7. The popular Japanese board game *Go* was actually invented in China around 400 BCE.
8. The Atari was the first dedicated home video game console.
9. Video games didn't include any kind of nudity until the 1990s, when the industry adopted a ratings system.
10. The first video game tournament was held in 1984.

MULTIPLE CHOICE

1. Role-playing games, in which players take on the role of characters in a fictional world, often use dice with more or fewer sides than the six-sided one common in modern board games. The first use of the 20-sided dice common in the hobby today was in:

A. China in 560 BCE
B. Mesoamerica in 50 CE
C. Ancient Egypt
D. Australia in 1823

2. Which video game was widely criticized for being "obscene" in regard to the sex scenes included, as part of a general wave of questioning the content and effect of video games on youth?

A. *Mass Effect*
B. *Syphon Filter*
C. *Soul Reaver*
D. *Metal Gear Solid*

3. The concept of using a 3D world and playing on a platform instead of a simple side-scroller has its origins in which decade?

A. 1990s
B. 1970s
C. 2000s
D. 1980s

4. Though ostensibly it has an "end game" criteria, there is no time limit set to reach the goal in which game, and gameplay can theoretically go on forever?

A. *Sorry*
B. Chinese checkers
C. *Monopoly*
D. *Pandemic*

5. While chess as we know it today originated in 15th century Europe, its roots are believed to be found in a very similar game called *Chaturanga* from when and where?

A. 12th century Ottoman Empire
B. 13th century Tenochtitlan
C. 7th century India
D. 6th century Ethiopia

ANSWER KEYS:

Music

TRUE OR FALSE

1. False. Mozart was a prolific composer with hundreds of works completed in his relatively short life.
2. True
3. True
4. False. Beethoven had a classical music education as a child. This story has no traceable origins.
5. False. Scientific studies have shown that low and high tempo songs both affect heart rate.
6. True
7. False. Neanderthals crafted a variety of simple instruments, such as flutes.
8. True
9. True
10. False. It was actually a general in the French army that owned the Stradivarius, which is frequently misattributed to Napoleon.

MULTIPLE CHOICE

1. B
2. D
3. A
4. A
5. D

Television

TRUE OR FALSE

1. True
2. False. It was actually a little-known show called *Mary Kay and Johnny* that ran from 1947–1950.
3. True
4. False. She was well-known for her physical comedy and played a large part in their planning.
5. True
6. True
7. False. The first television station was W2XB in New York, which began in 1928.
8. False. Color TV had been experimented with and desired from the very beginning.
9. True
10. False. The moon landing is still the most-watched event in television history, adjusting for population.

MULTIPLE CHOICE

1. D
2. C
3. A
4. D
5. A

Movies

TRUE OR FALSE

1. False. The first movie about the disaster, called *Saved from the Titanic*, was released only weeks after the event and starred actress Dorothy Gibson, who had actually been on board the ship.
2. True
3. False. The Nazis hated this movie and were known for public disruptions of screenings.
4. True
5. False. President Wilson loved the movie and had it shown more than once in the White House.
6. True.
7. True
8. False. The first sci-fi movie is *A Trip to the Moon*, made in 1902.
9. False. The cat was a stray that was found wandering the studio lot by director Francis Ford Coppola. The cat was so happy that its loud purring drowned out a lot of Brando's lines, and they had to be dubbed.
10. True

MULTIPLE CHOICE

1. C
2. C
3. A
4. D
5. B

Theatre

TRUE OR FALSE

1. True
2. False. Theaters were common in Britain, especially England.
3. True.
4. True
5. True
6. False. Pyrotechnics were used as far back as the Tudor era, if not earlier.
7. False. Among other rituals, many theaters will specifically leave a single light on the stage so that ghosts can perform at night and hopefully not interrupt performances.
8. True
9. False. *Phantom of the Opera* is the longest-running at 35 years.
10. False. He worked as a stage manager in London.

MULTIPLE CHOICE

1. C
2. A
3. D
4. C
5. A

Games

TRUE OR FALSE

1. False. Board games date back to ancient times, with many examples existing in ancient Egypt and Asia.
2. False. *Chiller* (1986) was the first.
3. True
4. True
5. False. There is some debate as to which was truly the first video game, but there are many early examples in the 1940s–1950s.
6. True
7. True
8. False. The first console was the Magnavox Odyssey in 1972.
9. False. *Softporn Adventure* in 1981 is considered to be the first.
10. False. The first tournament was in 1972 at Stanford University with the game being *Spacewar*.

MULTIPLE CHOICE

1. C
2. A
3. B
4. C
5. C

CHAPTER 6:
TRAVEL

TRAINS

TRUE OR FALSE

1. Railways evolved from horse-drawn carts running on rails into mines in the 16th century.
2. The first steam-powered locomotive was invented in 1848.
3. Cast iron was the preferred material for rails because of its strength and easy manufacturing.
4. The first passenger train pulled by a steam locomotive carried its travelers at a breakneck speed of eight miles per hour.
5. The first high-speed rail system, the Tōkaidō Shinkansen, began operations in Japan in 1964, connecting Tokyo and Osaka.
6. The first electric-powered locomotive was invented in 1902.
7. In the 19th century, the southern United States focused on building long, sprawling rail lines to link up cotton plantations across the open landscape.
8. The success of the first steam locomotives created a stock market bubble in England that came to be called "Railway Mania."
9. At the height of the rail travel boom in the early 20th century, there were only 15,000 miles of track in the United States because there were so few competing rail lines.
10. The world's fastest trains use electromagnets to levitate above the tracks.

MULTIPLE CHOICE

1. The first train station, which was originally for horse-drawn trains, was established in Wales in what year?

A. 1807
B. 1843
C. 1795
D. 1822

2. "Railway madness" was the colloquial term for:

A. A period of intense railway building in the 19th century
B. A stock bubble that burst which was brought on by dozens of new rail lines
C. A strange type of mania or nervous condition that affected some early train travelers
D. All of the above

3. Where is the world's longest monorail located?

A. China
B. Disney World
C. Brazil
D. Japan

4. Train robberies are a staple of Wild West stories, but the first recorded train robbery took place in which country?

A. Austria
B. France
C. Norway
D. England

5. What is a railway system for traveling steep slopes called?

A. Inclar
B. Funicular
C. Sloomesh
D. Rollech

AIR TRAVEL

TRUE OR FALSE

1. The earliest airlines offered no sort of refreshment on board their flights as it would add too much to the weight of the plane.
2. One in 5,000 long-distance flight travelers suffer from deep vein thrombosis, the third-most common vascular disease.
3. SpaceShipOne became the first privately funded aircraft to make a spaceflight on June 21, 2004.
4. Jet-powered aircraft weren't developed until after World War II, during the Cold War arms race.
5. Though he created the technical drawings in the 15th century, Leonardo da Vinci's famous "aerial screw" showed sound engineering and was technically capable of flight, yet was never built.
6. The idea of the modern aircraft as a machine with fixed wings, and separate systems for propulsion, control, and lift, was introduced in 1799 by Sir George Cayley.
7. The French, as avid fans of aviation, applauded early reports of the Wright Brothers' powered flight.
8. While the Hindenburg fire was not the first nor the most fatal airship accident, it was the first to be caught on a newsreel.
9. The first airline with fixed-wing craft and an actual schedule was established in 1923.
10. The first fatal aviation accident occurred in a Wright Model A aircraft on September 17, 1908, resulting in Orville Wright being injured, and the passenger Thomas Selfridge dying.

MULTIPLE CHOICE

1. While it remains unconfirmed if it actually happened, the origins of the term "Mile High Club" likely comes from a bet in an English gentleman's club in what year?

A. 1941
B. 1982
C. 1785
D. 1864

2. As of 2021, there were how many blimps left in the world, mainly used for advertisement?

A. 54
B. 16
C. 31
D. 25

3. A Boeing 747 uses how much fuel every second while in flight?

A. One gallon
B. 0.25 gallons
C. 2.5 gallons
D. 1.5 gallons

4. Though well-known for his aerial prowess in World War I, Manfred von Richthofen, or the "Red Baron" as he was commonly known, began his military service as:

A. An *aide de camp*
B. A cavalry officer
C. A munitions transporter
D. An infantryman

5. Amelia Earhart is well known for vanishing over the Pacific Ocean during her 1937 round-the-world flight, but in 1932 she completed what kind of flight?

A. Antarctic
B. Trans-Siberian
C. Trans-Atlantic
D. Tour of Africa

CARS

TRUE OR FALSE

1. The Toyota Corolla is the best-selling car series in history, dating back to 1966.
2. Stock car racing was founded after car prices fell drastically in the 1950s.
3. The first steam-powered automobile was invented in 1863.
4. The word "car" ultimately derives from the Gaulish word *karros* meaning "chariot."
5. Electric cars with rechargeable engines were invented in 1972 during the Gas Crisis in the United States.
6. Despite the fad for nuclear-powered everything in the Atomic Age, there were never any plans for nuclear-powered cars.
7. Bertha Bentz, the business partner, investor, and wife of automobile inventor Carl Benz, became the world's first automobile long-distance driver while field testing the patent prototype for her husband's car design.
8. Though automobiles had been around for some time, the first organized race wasn't held until 1919.
9. Henry Ford's famous assembly line-style of manufacturing was inspired by the large-scale butchers in the Chicago area that worked in the same manner.
10. Anti-lock braking systems were invented in the 1980s and were later adapted to help improve train braking.

MULTIPLE CHOICE

1. Formula One driver Lella Lombardi is the only woman to have scored in the:

A. Indy 500
B. Portuguese Grand Prix
C. World Championship
D. Tour de France

2. While internal combustion cars convert about 15% of their fuel to movement, electric cars convert what percentage of the released electric current into forward motion?

A. 10%
B. 21%
C. 36%
D. 77%

3. In 2020, the first of what type of car was introduced?

A. Self-driving taxis
B. Hydrogen-fueled cars
C. Bullet proof consumer cars
D. Airplane conversion cars

4. The first patent application for what car feature was filed in 1845?

A. Wind shields
B. Block and pulley breaks
C. Rubber tires
D. A gear box

5. In the United States, as well as in the United Kingdom, it was necessary for early car owners to do what to warn owners of horses and livestock that an automobile was approaching?

A. Honk their horn every five minutes
B. Wave a red flag no less than 60 yards in front of the vehicle
C. Stop at every intersection and step out to call attention to themselves
D. Launch a flare upon entering a town

SHIPS AND BOATS

TRUE OR FALSE

1. The Swedish warship *Vasa*, built between 1626 and 1628 to be the flagship of the Swedish Navy, sank on her maiden voyage having only sailed just short of a mile.
2. The HMS *Terror*, a British warship refitted for arctic expeditions almost sank from iceberg-related damages on its return from the arctic. She then set out on her second and last arctic expedition, where she was abandoned after becoming stuck in the ice.
3. A German U-boat fired on the civilian *Lusitania* ship with no prior warning in 1915.
4. Ironclad warships were first used in a skirmish between Britain and France over the rights to a colony in Africa.
5. The first ships to be propelled with sail and three sets of oars, replacing the older ships with only two sets of oars, first appeared at the end of the 8th century BCE.
6. The US Navy didn't begin researching nuclear-powered submarines until the 1950s after it became clear that the Soviet Union was looking into atomic submarines.
7. The *Gerald R. Ford* aircraft carrier is outfitted with as many aircraft as the whole air force of Sweden.
8. The first recorded submarine was demonstrated in the river Tagus near Toledo in 1562.
9. The concept of a cruise ship exclusively for pleasure wasn't developed until the 1900s when sailing became faster and safer.
10. Viking longships were heavy and difficult to maneuver.

MULTIPLE CHOICE

1. Since its invention in 1922, water skiing has developed into an international sport with how many different events?

A. Two
B. Seven
C. Five
D. Three

2. The *Titanic* carried a total of how many tons of coal when she pulled out of port?

A. 7,703 tons
B. 10,000 tons
C. 2506 tons
D. 3612 tons

3. The Confederate American States submarine *H. L. Hunley* did what three times?

A. Ran out of fuel at sea
B. Had its weapons switched out
C. Sank
D. Single-handedly achieved major victory

4. Disney's largest cruise ship can accommodate up to 4,000 passengers in its how many staterooms?

A. 1,156
B. 1,254
C. 1,300
D. 1,765

5. While they see use outside of submarines, the periscope was first used in an underwater vehicle in what year?

A. 1798
B. 1834
C. 1886
D. 1919

UNMOTORIZED

TRUE OR FALSE

1. The stagecoach, or *diligence* in French, became a popular method of conveyance for passengers and mail all over Europe, North America, and Australia in the days before the invention of the railroad.
2. All velocipedes are bicycles.
3. The Romans adopted chariots into the military in honor of the Greeks, whom they revered.
4. The first bicycle traffic accident to be recorded occurred in Glasgow in 1842 when a man knocked over a young girl and was fined five shillings for the offense.
5. Skateboarding originates in the 19th century when delivery boys, bored between assignments, would put pieces of crates on top of steel pipes and race them.
6. The indigenous population of Peru has a history of using personal reed watercraft for surfing the waves of the South American coast, while fishing.
7. Roller Derby is a full-contact sport played by roller skating around a track. One member from each team attempts to get past the remaining members of the opposing team to score.
8. Kick scooters were developed in the 1980s with the rise in popularity of roller skating.
9. The fastest journey by inline skates across the mainland United States took 62 days.
10. While invented for stage performances in the 18th century, roller skates did not see widespread use until the 1840s.

MULTIPLE CHOICE

1. The Giro d'Italia is a multistage, long distance race in which the competitors use what to reach the finish line?

A. Roller skates
B. Bikes
C. Roller skis
D. All of the above

2. In 1999, the United States Marine Corps tested commercially available skateboards as a means to do what during urban combat?

A. Improve advancing speed through the streets
B. Perform non-motorized drive-by ambushes
C. Facilitate munitions transport
D. Detect tripwires and snipers, and maneuver inside buildings.

3. When the bike became affordable and commonplace in 1890s Europe and North America, it contributed to the liberation of women, particularly:

A. Upper and middle-class White women
B. Lower class women of all races
C. Black women
D. Older women of all social classes

4. Wild water racing is a type of river race where the object is to traverse a set distance in a churning river as fast as possible using what craft?

A. Surfboard
B. Rowboat
C. Canoe
D. Inflatable raft

5. Biathlon is a winter sports event that combines what with cross-country skiing?

A. Ski jumping
B. Rifle marksmanship
C. Downhill races
D. Archery

ANSWER KEYS:

Trains

TRUE OR FALSE

1. True
2. False. The first locomotive capable of carrying people made its first journey on February 21, 1804.
3. False. Cast iron was quite brittle and didn't move or flex well enough to be used for rails.
4. True
5. True
6. False. The first electric rail transport was built in 1837 by a Scotsman named Robert Aberdeen.
7. False. Rail lines in the South were generally very short, only linking up close communities. This was a major setback for them during the Civil War.
8. True
9. False. There were over 250,000 miles of track at the peak around 1900.
10. True

MULTIPLE CHOICE

1. A
2. C
3. A
4. D
5. B

Air Travel

TRUE OR FALSE

1. False. Food and drink were always integral parts of air travel, with many airlines offering large, luxurious meals with multiple courses to attract customers.
2. True
3. True
4. False. The first jet was tested in 1939 by German scientist Heinkel He.
5. False. The aerial screw would, at best, only be capable of a sort of controlled descent as drawn and with the materials available at the time.
6. True
7. False. The French were generally quite hostile to the Wright Brothers, with many accusing them of lying about the distance of their flight - or that they flew at all!
8. True
9. True
10. False

MULTIPLE CHOICE

1. C
2. D
3. A
4. B
5. C

Cars

TRUE OR FALSE

1. True
2. False. Stock car racing originated in the 1920s-30s with bootleggers during Prohibition. Races began being organized soon after.
3. False. The first steam vehicle that worked reliably and could carry a person was invented in 1801 by Richard Trevithick.
4. True
5. False. The first truly electric automobile is generally accepted to be the Flocken Elektrowagon built in 1888.
6. False. There were actually several proposals for nuclear-powered cars (a form of steam car, actually), but fears about safety following accidents and the bombings of Japan in WWII shelved that notion.
7. True
8. False. Racing has been around for as long as there have been vehicles. The first planned race took place in 1867 in England.
9. True
10. False. It was the other way around - train braking systems influenced the invention of anti-lock brakes on cars and began to be put on some car models in the 1950s, though they were rare and not always efficient.

MULTIPLE CHOICE

1. C
2. D
3. A
4. C
5. B

Ships and Boats

TRUE OR FALSE

1. True
2. True
3. False. The Germans actually gave several warnings, including full-page newspaper announcements before the ship even departed.
4. False. Though France and Britain engaged in a kind of ship-building race in the 1840s, battles between ironclad ships happened in the 1860s during the American Civil War.
5. True
6. False. The idea was first suggested in 1939.
7. True
8. True
9. False. Cruise ships purely built for pleasure date back to at least the 1600s in Europe.
10. False. Viking longships were actually very light and agile for their size due to their clever construction and use of materials. Many were light enough to pull up on shore and be carried across land by the crew if needed.

MULTIPLE CHOICE

1. D
2. A
3. C
4. B
5. B

Unmotorized

TRUE OR FALSE

1. True
2. False. A velocipede can take many shapes, including tricycles and other wheeled vehicles that are essentially foot powered.
3. False. The Romans only used chariots for sport, with chariot races being a common event in coliseums throughout the empire.
4. True
5. False. Skateboarding originated in the 1940s or 1950s in California as a way for surfers to have fun while the ocean was flat.
6. True
7. True
8. False. Kick scooters have been around since at least the 1920s, frequently being homemade.
9. False. Kacie Fisher completed a journey across the United States in only 47 days in 2012.
10. True

MULTIPLE CHOICE

1. B
2. D
3. A
4. C
5. B

CHAPTER 7:
EARLY MODERN HISTORY

MEDIEVAL EUROPE

TRUE OR FALSE

1. Bathing was discouraged in medieval times, as it was thought that germs entered the body through regular washing of any kind.
2. Animals could be tried for crimes, including murder, and were sometimes sentenced to death in medieval Europe.
3. The most common means that people in medieval Europe believed witches used to travel was via broomstick.
4. Because England couldn't afford to keep a large standing army, it was once compulsory for all men of fighting age to attend weekly (or more frequent) archery practice.
5. People on pilgrimage frequently acted without regard to normal morality standards because they had a sort of spiritual "immunity" by virtue of their trip's purpose.
6. Many edicts had to be read from the pulpit in Britain because so many people were sneaking into churches to have sex as they were often the only non-residential buildings in most communities.
7. The most common sentence for those accused of witchcraft in medieval Europe was to be burnt at the stake.
8. Hildegard von Bingen wrote an early treatise on birth control.
9. It was commonly believed in the medieval period that women had a higher sex drive than men.
10. Chaucer was an early advocate for the Reformation, as seen in the more critical passages of *The Canterbury Tales.*

MULTIPLE CHOICE

1. In 1314, King Edward II of England became the first of many English kings to attempt to ban what sport, as it was seen as a distraction from work and other duties the citizens had?

A. Tennis
B. Cricket
C. Golf
D. Soccer

2. As descriptors of human personality, the 'four humors' relate to:

A. Methods of comedic acting
B. The fluids blood, phlegm, black bile, and yellow bile
C. The bones in the upper arms and the thighs, and their length,

D. The four seasons, and their dominance in a person

3. The fate of women in medieval Europe is commonly thought of as one of servitude with no rights. In the early medieval period, however, women had some control of what, based on Roman and Germanic law?

A. Their own business
B. Their religious attendance
C. Their own children
D. Their own dowry, marriage, and property

4. In addition to covering their hair for beauty purposes, medieval women also did what?

A. Plucked their hairlines
B. Flattened their noses
C. Made their cheeks wider by putting wool inside them
D. Stretched their earlobes

5. What was the Erfurt latrine disaster in 1184 caused by?

A. A herd of frightened cows stampeding through the city breaking many latrines and spilling the contents
B. The assembled nobles of the Holy Roman Empire breaking through the floor of the cathedral provostry and falling into the cesspit below.
C. Angry peasants pelting the mayor's home with excrement for a whole week
D. The latrine emptiers going on an early form of workers' strike and refusing to empty the latrines until their demands were met, which happened a month later.

THE RENAISSANCE

TRUE OR FALSE

1. Henry VIII of England was deeply inspired by the Renaissance in Italy and wished to bring many of its aesthetics and schools of thought to England in the early part of his reign.
2. Renaissance scholars sought to understand historical texts from Classical antiquity rather than simply to resolve contradictions between said authors.
3. It was considered heretical to study texts from the Muslim and Arabic-speaking world.
4. Unlike during the Medieval period, women during the Renaissance largely enjoyed a great deal of freedom and the right to own property on their own.
5. Despite common portrayals, fashionable women weren't slathering themselves in stark white face paint - the recipes commonly used produced a subtle, delicate blurring effect.
6. Pork rinds were a popular snack among the aristocracy.
7. Pope Sixtus V declared the Roman Colosseum a protected landmark that should be preserved at all costs.
8. Double-entry bookkeeping was integral to the financial growth of the Renaissance.
9. Niccolo Machiavelli admonished people to leave their destinies up to Fortune, as this was what was counseled by the Catholic Church at the time.
10. Significant evidence suggests that many Renaissance artists used a *camera obscura* to achieve their distinctly realistic style.

MULTIPLE CHOICE

1. The laws in many European nations that governed who could wear what in terms of fabric, color, amount of decorations, etc., were referred to as:

A. Garment law
B. Linen legislation
C. Sumptuary laws
D. Shirt-and-skirt regulation

2. Though more known for his art and inventions, during his lifetime, Leonardo da Vinci was also known as an accomplished what?

A. Lyre player
B. Dancer
C. Tailor
D. Cook

3. What does the term "Renaissance" actually mean?

A. The time of learning
B. Rebirth
C. Questioning
D. Artistry

4. The first wave of the Renaissance was centered around a new philosophy called what?

A. Animalism
B. Cosmology
C. Planescaping
D. Humanism

5. Many cosmetics texts in the mid-to-late Renaissance, which were usually in the keeping of physicians and alchemists, include recipes for:

A. Lightening women's hair
B. Lipstick in fantastic colors
C. Body paint
D. Tooth dyes

THE ENLIGHTENMENT

TRUE OR FALSE

1. Garden hermits were fashionable during the period, living on the estates of the noble and wealthy and expected to play their part convincingly.
2. The Enlightenment was preceded by and overlapped with the Scientific Revolution.
3. Marie Antoinette famously rejected all ideals of the Enlightenment.
4. The last person to be executed for witchcraft in Scotland was Janet Horne in 1727.
5. The Age of Enlightenment saw many philosophical changes, but it was firmly believed that the Church should continue to have a place in government and legal proceedings.
6. Women had very little effect on promoting ideas of the Enlightenment.
7. Eastern philosophers were the main inspiration for the Age of Reason.
8. Thomas Jefferson's nail factory employed almost exclusively enslaved children.
9. During the American Revolution, many British soldiers put on plays on Broadway in their downtime.
10. Sir Isaac Newton, famed as a physicist today, was also a mathematician, astronomer, theologist, and alchemist.

MULTIPLE CHOICE

1. Many date the beginning of the Age of Enlightenment to 1637, when René Descartes published which work, which features the famous phrase, "I think, therefore I am"?

A. *To Think Humanly*
B. *An Examination of Society through Logic*
C. *Discourse on the Method*
D. *Philosophies for a New World*

2. Enlightenment ideals spread quickly and voraciously partly due to what venues, which by their nature and setup had a naturally egalitarian approach to debate?

A. Coffee houses
B. Public libraries
C. The first open-air parks
D. Galleries that opened to the public

3. Despite his retrospective contribution to the Enlightenment, the works of which philosopher were largely ignored during his lifetime and were occasionally even openly ridiculed?

A. Immanuel Kant
B. Francis Bacon
C. Benjamin Franklin
D. John Locke

4. Many Enlightenment philosophers had backgrounds in which field?

A. Literature
B. The arts
C. Science
D. Mathematics

5. One of the hallmarks of the Enlightenment (which partially allowed it to spread so quickly) was which new concept?

A. The public sphere, wherein physical space, printed media, and other aspects of society were available to the public as a whole
B. Prioritizing education for girls so that they could achieve parity with young men
C. Enfranchising all voting-age men, regardless of income and race so that the true measure of a country could be taken
D. Opening government legislation to the public so that they could more easily comment and decide on important matters

THE INDUSTRIAL REVOLUTION

TRUE OR FALSE

1. While commonly associated with the 1800s, the Industrial Revolution began in England in 1760.
2. The entrepreneurial spirit and early consumerism that drove industrialization in England first spread to Belgium, shortly followed by France and the United States.
3. Though often talked about, and undoubtedly important, the Industrial Revolution still pales in importance when compared to the Agricultural Revolution several thousand years earlier.
4. With the rise of industry in England, city populations began an unprecedented and sustained growth.
5. Even though the accumulation and spending of wealth have been a driving force throughout human history, it would take a long time for a true capitalist economy to manifest in the wake of the Industrial Revolution.
6. The absence of labor laws caused factories to have a high frequency of accidents, many of which caused mutilation and death, even among child workers.
7. The increased availability of cheap consumer goods and building materials caused living standards to increase significantly with larger and cleaner homes for all workers.
8. Though some people did move to the cities to work in the new factories, cities mostly already had the workforce they needed to fill the factories that were being built.
9. During the Industrial Revolution the rate of literacy dropped sharply as children were taken out of schools to provide more income by working in factories.
10. Since the new industrial machines did most of the heavy labor involved in the manufacture of goods, the status of women rose steadily during the Industrial Revolution since they could now perform the same tasks as men.

MULTIPLE CHOICE

1. What was the first industrial machine, a textile manufacturing device, called?

A. Knitting Amanda
B. Cutting Carl
C. Spinning Jenny
D. Weaving Albert

2. What were the anti-industrialization activists who opposed workers being replaced by machines called?

A. Floppers
B. Smackers
C. Rackites
D. Luddites

3. Puerperal madness was a label applied to women in 19th century that did what, and was used as a means to explain why the "angel in the house" could do such a thing?

A. Committed infanticide
B. Went on shoplifting sprees
C. Dedicated themselves to sexual pleasure
D. Wanted to perform heavy manual labor

4. The *Mines and Collieries Act* of 1842 was partly in reaction to a mining disaster in which child workers were killed, but also due to newspaper articles showing what?

A. The cruel working conditions of pit ponies
B. Shirtless women working in the mines
C. The workers being forced to work on Sundays
D. The workers' poor diets

5. As agriculture was industrialized, which innovations was both loved and loathed by the workers, as they made their jobs easier, but also reduced the number of workers needed?

A. New methods of plowing that took soil drainage into account
B. The rise of animal inoculations
C. New chemical fertilizers
D. Threshing machines

THE REFORMATION

TRUE OR FALSE

1. Martin Luther, the founder of the Protestant Reformation, was a professor of Moral Theology at the University of Wittenberg at the time that he published his 95 Theses.
2. All three of the Defenestrations of Prague were the result of disagreements between Reformationist and counter-Reformationist supporters.
3. Perhaps the most famous monarch associated with the Reformation, Henry VIII remained a staunch supporter of the movement even on his deathbed.
4. Martin Luther married the reformed former nun, Katharina von Bora, and together they had six children.
5. Once England had rejected the Catholic faith, it would never become the official religion of England again.
6. Martin Luther was fond of the game of bowling, so much so that he had a private lane built next to his house.
7. The Puritans were seen as religious fanatics and many of them were persecuted, prosecuted, or had their property seized.
8. The Reformation was slow to spread from Germany.
9. Though Henry VIII was motivated by his desire to marry Anne Boleyn, it was equally important to him that he seize the property owned by the Catholic Church as Britain's finances were not robust.
10. The Reformation spread mostly via word of mouth, with many of its supporters reluctant to publish works on the new printing presses.

MULTIPLE CHOICE

1. One of Martin Luther's key beliefs at the time of the Reformation was that the leaders of the Catholic church had fundamentally misunderstood and misinterpreted what?

A. The Sermon on the Mount
B. The 10 Commandments
C. The Book of Psalms
D. The Bible as a whole

2. The invention of what in the 1400s is credited with the teachings of Martin Luther becoming widespread across Europe?

A. Postal system
B. Carrier pigeons
C. Printing press
D. Paperback books

3. At the height of the Reformation, a scholar named William Tyndale translated the Bible into English for the first time. What happened to him as a result?

A. He was knighted by Elizabeth I
B. He was made Archbishop of Canterbury
C. He was made president of Oxford University
D. He was executed

4. Which of these minor branches of Christianity was the principal religion of Switzerland during the Reformation era?

A. Mormonism
B. Calvinism
C. Lutheranism
D. Anglicanism

5. How long did the Reformation era's Thirty-Years War actually last?

A. 30 days
B. 10 years
C. 29 years
D. 30 years

ANSWER KEYS:

Medieval Europe

TRUE OR FALSE

1. False. Cleanliness was highly encouraged by every major religion, and public baths were available throughout Europe, especially at cathedrals and major stops on pilgrim routes.
2. True
3. False. The most common way that witches allegedly traveled was riding animals or transforming themselves into animals.
4. True
5. True
6. True
7. False. Witches were only burned if they were accused of heresy as well, which was rare up until later in the 16th century. The most common way they were executed was via hanging.
8. False. While Hildegard von Bingen wrote prolifically, she was a Catholic nun, and would therefore not have been in favor of birth control.
9. True
10. False. Though he could at times be critical of corruption found within Catholicism, he died far before the Reformation even began.

MULTIPLE CHOICE

1. D
2. B
3. D
4. A
5. B

The Renaissance

TRUE OR FALSE

1. True
2. True
3. False. The Renaissance owed much to these texts and the Arabic-speaking world in general.
4. False. Women were still mostly treated as their husband's property and could not own anything of their own with few exceptions.
5. True
6. True
7. False. Sixtus V actually wanted to tear part of it down to make way for needed industry, or to at least utilize part of it for wool preparation.
8. True
9. True
10. True

MULTIPLE CHOICE

1. C
2. A
3. B
4. D
5. A

The Enlightenment

TRUE OR FALSE

1. True
2. True
3. False. She was interested in the ideals and held social gatherings where her guests could learn about and discuss them.
4. True
5. False. Enlightenment ideas prominently considered religion to not have a place in politics.
6. False. Fashionable women would host salons and other gatherings where ideas were exchanged and philosophers discussed their work. It was largely thanks to these parties that Enlightenment ideas could spread.
7. False. The main inspirations were texts from Classical antiquity.
8. True
9. True
10. True

MULTIPLE CHOICE

1. C
2. A
3. D
4. C
5. A

The Industrial Revolution

TRUE OR FALSE

1. True
2. True
3. False. The Industrial Revolution has had the greatest impact on how humans live compared to all others in history.
4. True
5. False. A capitalist economy followed quickly in the wake of industrial development.
6. True
7. False. While mass-produced goods of all kinds became available, poverty was rampant among the lower classes.
8. False. The creation of factory work opportunities caused people in rural areas to migrate to the cities in vast numbers.
9. True
10. False. Women actually lost status. As many jobs they had traditionally done were taken over by machines, their value in society dropped.

MULTIPLE CHOICE

1. C
2. D
3. A
4. B
5. D

The Reformation

TRUE OR FALSE

1. True
2. False. Only the third act of throwing someone out a window was connected to the Reformation.
3. False. Henry VIII demanded a Catholic confession on his deathbed.
4. True
5. False. Catholics and Protestants fought for control, with the official religion switching back to Catholicism depending on who sat on the throne.
6. True
7. True
8. False. The Reformation ideas spread like wildfire but were not without opposition.
9. True
10. False. The rise in literacy thanks to the printing press was integral to spreading the message, and reformationists happily printed many publications on their new ideas.

MULTIPLE CHOICE

1. D
2. C
3. D
4. B
5. D

CHAPTER 8:
DRINK

BEER

TRUE OR FALSE

1. The oldest evidence of beer brewing is 13,000 years old.
2. Early European beer contained strictly grains to avoid wasting any valuable foodstuffs.
3. Hops were added to beer to help prevent it from spoiling, not to help with the flavor.
4. Beer brewing was considered a domestic activity until the late Medieval period.
5. The Industrial Revolution had little impact on the brewing industry besides changing the volume of beer that could be produced and shipped.
6. The Joseph Schlitz Brewing Company was the first in the world to begin using brown bottles for beer.
7. The first case of post-Prohibition beer produced by Budweiser was delivered by its famous Clydesdale horses, which was their introduction to the world.
8. Despite the prolific brewing industry, beer is only the fifth most popular drink in the world, following water, tea, coffee, and Coca-Cola.
9. To help beer retain its fizz, it was originally bottled with raisins in it.
10. Though its population is larger in number, China consumes less than half of the beer that the United States does.

MULTIPLE CHOICE

1. The earliest example of beer being mentioned in writing is from ancient Egypt, but there is archaeological evidence of beer making from which date—though we would probably not recognize it as beer today?

A. 7000 BCE
B. 9000 BCE
C. 11000 BCE
D. 13000 BCE

2. Commonly called "liquid bread," the actual nutritional value of beer depends on the kind of what used?

A. Yeast
B. Grain
C. Fermentation process
D. All of the above

3. The beer cocktail known as "Black Velvet" is a layered drink that combines which of the following two ingredients?

A. Ale and cognac
B. Porter and rum
C. Stout and mango juice
D. Stout and sparkling wine

4. What country has the lowest beer consumption rate in the world, with only 23.67 ounces per person per year?

A. Kenya
B. Indonesia
C. Brazil
D. Israel

5. The hops used in beer is a type of what?

A. Pine
B. Hemp
C. Peony
D. Weed

WINE

TRUE OR FALSE

1. Upon his death, Alexander the Great had wine from his homeland put into his coffin with him, which acted as a preservative.
2. Bordeaux mixture, a combination of copper sulfate and quicklime that is used to prevent pests and fungus on grapevines, was first used to keep passers-by from eating grapes right off the vine because of the bitter taste.
3. Red wine was associated with blood in ancient Egypt and featured in some of their religious ceremonies.
4. There were over 1,500 bottles of wine on the RMS *Titanic* when it sank.
5. The Aztec Empire had a thriving wine industry, which the Spanish conquistadors used to their advantage.
6. Wine fraud is a purely modern crime, as most ancient cultures considered it an affront to various alcohol-adjacent deities, such as Bacchus.
7. In Thailand, it is common to add salted peanuts to wine as a snack.
8. Before the Islamic Revolution in 1979, Iran had a thriving wine industry and was a major exporter.
9. As much as 50% of all wine bottle corks come from Portugal.
10. The fear or hatred of wine is called oenophobia.

MULTIPLE CHOICE

1. A wine collection from Château d'Yquem, spanning every vintage from 1860 to 2003, was sold for how much?

A. $500,000
B. $1.5 million
C. $2.3 million
D. $8 million

2. The ideal wine cellar temperature is between what range degrees Fahrenheit?

A. 41 and 46.4
B. 53.6 and 57.2
C. 64.4 and 78.8
D. 50 and 59

3. Wine consumption in France accounts for what percentage of their total alcohol consumption?

A. 29.7%
B. 32%
C. 56.8%
D. 77.8%

4. The most expensive wine ever was a bottle 1945 Romanée-Conti, which sold for how much in an auction in Switzerland?

A. $558,000
B. $769,000
C. $872,000
D. $297,000

5. In Ancient Rome, what substance sometimes accidentally ended up in wine, because the fruit syrups used to sweeten it were typically prepared in vessels made from it?

A. Terracotta clay
B. Lead
C. Gold
D. Potash

TRADITIONAL DRINKS

TRUE OR FALSE

1. Hong Kong-style milk tea is considered an Intangible Cultural Heritage by the United Nations.
2. Kvass is a common Russian fermented non-alcoholic beverage made from rye bread.
3. Though rum is a major export from the Caribbean nation of Antigua and Barbuda, the drink is not popular among its people.
4. Tequila is named after the Mexican bishop and hobbyist distiller Manuel Tequila, who first made it in 1824.
5. In Botswana, ginger beer is a popular homemade non-alcoholic drink served on festive occasions.
6. Due to a flourishing camel-breeding industry in Australia, fermented camel milk has become a drink enjoyed throughout the nation.
7. Coconut water is the national drink of the Republic of the Marshall Islands.
8. Since its introduction to the Republic of Macedonia in the 1950s, the low alcohol and carbonated orange drink Skalli has become popular at all levels of society.
9. Spiced apple cider is the traditional drink served in Sweden at Christmas.
10. The Canadian cocktail called Caesar is identical to a Bloody Mary, except for the addition of hot clam broth.

MULTIPLE CHOICE

1. The tequila worm is:

A. Important for flavor
B. Added as a marketing gimmick
C. A tradition connected to coming of age rituals
D. A sign of poor pest control in the distillery

2. What is the name of the drink brewed by the indigenous peoples of Brazil, made from fermented corn or manioc?

A. Cauim
B. Blodool
C. Raquim
D. Falcata

3. Arak, a drink originating in the Levantine, is made from grapes and what other ingredient?

A. Cumin
B. Cardamom
C. Turmeric
D. Aniseed

4. Who is it traditional for saké to be served by?

A. The host
B. The hostess
C. All participants to each other
D. Oneself

5. With origins in central Mexico, what is the name of a thick, milk-white drink made from fermented agave plant sap?

A. Mezcal
B. Pulque
C. Sangria
D. Tamarindo

UNUSUAL DRINKS

TRUE OR FALSE

1. Vine-Glo was a solid grape concentrate, usually sold in brick-form, that was popular during the Prohibition Era in the United States because the instructions had very detailed instructions on how *not* to make it into wine.
2. In Thailand, whiskey is made with herbs and powdered reindeer antlers added for flavor.
3. *Kalcha* is a drink from India made by adding spider venom to distilled millet beer. The spider venom is neutralized by the alcohol.
4. The Aunt Roberta cocktail from Alabama in the United States is a potent concoction that blends brandy with vodka, absinthe, gin, and blackberry liqueur.
5. *Mashasha* is a fermented drink common throughout the central parts of Africa made from fish guts and green mold.
6. *Durlaga* is a cocktail from India made from turmeric, dragon fruit, and rice alcohol.
7. *Boza* is a common drink in Bulgaria and the Caucasus that is made from fermenting boiled flour. It is popular with children and recommended to pregnant women to stimulate milk production.
8. Arctic indigenous tribes consume a drink of fermented seaweed and tundra lichen.
9. Northern Europeans would purposefully hunt female animals in the Neolithic age just so that they could harvest milk from them to ferment.
10. The national drink of the Dominican Republic, called *mamajuana*, has no single recipe and is often sold as an aphrodisiac.

MULTIPLE CHOICE

1. The *aragog* served in Mexico City is made from Mexican *mezcal*, Brazilian *cachaca*, mango juice, Chilean *pisco*, a touch of lemon, and what else?

A. A spoon of breast milk
B. A sprinkling of coconut
C. A fermented tapeworm
D. A drop of tarantula venom

2. *Kumis* is a drink traditional to central Asia that is made from fermented what?

A. Cow's milk
B. Steppe grass
C. Mare's milk
D. Peat moss

3. In Korea, *soju*, a fermented rice drink, is sometimes thickened with what ingredient?

A. Gelatin derived from octopus tentacles
B. Calf's foot jelly
C. Fluid from a tuna's eye
D. Boiled pig snouts

4. *Mezcal de pechuga*, unlike regular *mezcal*, has which extra special ingredient?

A. Raw poultry hung over the brewing still
B. Ground worms added in the aging stage
C. Calf bones added while brewing
D. A piece of leather added just before bottling

5. Baby Mice Wine is made by dropping a handful of live three-day old mice into rice wine and leaving it to sit. What is it claimed to taste like?

A. Vanilla and tar
B. Gasoline
C. Sweat and sugar
D. Asphalt

NON-ALCOHOLIC

TRUE OR FALSE

1. Coca-Cola is still made with leaves from the coca plant (from which cocaine is derived) today.
2. Welch's famous grape juice was originally made as an alternative to using wine in Protestant religious services.
3. Mineralized natural spring water is a popular drink throughout South America.
4. Orange juice has a comparable amount of sugar to sodas.
5. Sprite was originally developed in California in the 1940s as a way to capitalize on the citrus industry in the state.
6. The root beer float, made by adding vanilla ice cream to root beer, is called not because of the floating ice cream but in reference to Castos' floating bar and restaurant on the Mississippi River where it was first served.
7. The first bottled water factory was established in 1622 at the Holy Well in Malvern Hills.
8. In 1960, Dr Pepper promoted the idea of serving the soft drink hot with lemon slices in winter to help chase away the cold.
9. PepsiCo was founded by a disgruntled former employee of the Coca-Cola company who took the secret of cola drinks with him when he left.
10. We know the Sumerians had a thriving fruit juice market from the volume of clay tablets with customer complaints about the quality of the juice in question!

MULTIPLE CHOICE

1. *Warugaki* is a Japanese drink made from fruit juice, caramel coloring, and malt extract. What is it often called?

A. American Cola
B. Kid's Beer
C. Fizzy Fun
D. Poorman's Beer

2. In 2023, no less than how many metric tons of coffee beans were produced worldwide?

A. 7,634,925
B. 6,728,032
C. 5,273,160
D. 9,428,761

3. Despite being slightly acidic, it would take 100 years of daily consumption of carbonated water to cause damage to which part of the body?

A. Teeth
B. Stomach lining
C. Kidneys
D. Esophagus

4. Taurin, first discovered in 1827 in ox bile...:

A. Is naturally produced by the human liver
B. Has no benefits when consumed
C. Is a common ingredient in energy drinks
D. All of the above

5. Though they are a non-alcoholic treat today, originally milkshakes were made with which of these ingredient combinations?

A. Eggs, milk, whiskey, and sugar or sweet syrups
B. Whipped egg whites, cherry cordial, and gin
C. Vodka, heavy cream, sugar, and cinnamon
D. Milk, rosewater, egg yolks, and rum

ANSWER KEYS:

Beer

TRUE OR FALSE

1. True
2. False. Early European beer contained spices, fruits, honey, and other flavorings in varying degrees.
3. True
4. True
5. False. Industrial beer dominated the market, punching out artisanal beer entirely.
6. True
7. True
8. False. Beer is the third-most popular drink, after water and tea.
9. False. Raisins are sometimes used in the making of Champagne bubbles, but never in beer.
10. False. China consumes roughly double the amount that the US does annually.

MULTIPLE CHOICE

1. C
2. D
3. D
4. B
5. B

Wine

TRUE OR FALSE

1. False. His sarcophagus was filled with honey.
2. True
3. True
4. True
5. False. Although there was a species of grapes that was used for food, it was never made into wine until after colonization.
6. False. Wine fraud has existed for about as long as wine has, with people adding everything from water to dangerous chemicals and dyes.
7. False. While there has been a growing fad for eating salted peanuts with wine (perhaps even putting them *in* the wine), this has never been a snack associated with Thailand.
8. True
9. True
10. True

MULTIPLE CHOICE

1. B
2. D
3. C
4. A
5. B

Traditional Drinks

TRUE OR FALSE

1. True
2. True
3. False. Rum is the national drink of Antigua and Barbuda.
4. False. Tequila is named for its region of origin, as are so many other distinct alcoholic drinks.
5. True
6. False. Though camels are raised and exported from Australia, their milk is not fermented and drunk.
7. True
8. False. No drink of that name exists.
9. False. Mulled wine is common, not spiced apple cider.
10. True

MULTIPLE CHOICE

1. B
2. A
3. A
4. C
5. B

Unusual Drinks

TRUE OR FALSE

1. True
2. True
3. False. No such drink exists, but snake venom in alcohol is common in traditional Chinese medicine.
4. True
5. False. Mashasha is a musical artist from Zimbabwe.
6. False. Durlaga is a village in India close to a regional airport.
7. True
8. False. Though this drink doesn't exist, there is one that results from letting a seagull ferment in water.
9. False. There is no evidence of Neolithic hunters targeting prey of one sex over another.
10. True

MULTIPLE CHOICE

1. D
2. C
3. C
4. A
5. B

Non-Alcoholic

TRUE OR FALSE

1. True
2. True
3. False. Instead, tea made from dried Yerba Mate leaves is common.
4. True
5. False. It was created in 1955 in Houston, and it had strawberry and orange flavors.
6. False. The root beer float is indeed named for the ice cream floating in it.
7. True
8. True
9. False. It was founded by a pharmacist after the business of selling the cola drink he developed took off.
10. False. The Sumerians did, however, leave many clay tablets complaining about the quality of copper that was sold by some merchants.

MULTIPLE CHOICE

1. B
2. C
3. A
4. D
5. A

CHAPTER 9:
DRESS

UNMENTIONABLES

TRUE OR FALSE

1. The concept of women's underwear that had a closed seam and actually covered the crotch area is relatively recent, only gaining popularity in the 1910s.
2. Corsets were restrictive garments, pulling the waist in painfully and affecting internal organs.
3. Patterned silk stockings were fashionable in men's clothing during the 1700s and were referred to as "clocked."
4. In Western fashion, men didn't have dedicated underwear unless it was very cold; instead, they would wear long shirts, which were then tucked into breeches and around their crotch to act as underwear.
5. In the 1600s, a fad for bronzed bodices, or "pair of bodies" as they were known, spread from Italy through the rest of Europe.
6. Before the invention of the bra, there was no real way to enhance a woman's bust because of the restrictive nature of undergarments.
7. Without elastic, women would use ribbons tied just below the knee to keep their stockings from falling down.
8. Bras are a thoroughly modern invention, with women either having unsupported breasts or some form of boned bodice like a corset to act as support before their inception.
9. In the 1940s, during the rationing of World War II, women would use makeup pencils on a stirrup-shaped holder to draw lines on the back of their bare legs so that it would look like they were actually wearing silk stockings.
10. The bullet bra referred to World War II bombs and was seen as part of a patriotic look during the war.

MULTIPLE CHOICE

1. Men's boxer shorts are commonly cited as being better for sperm production, but there is also growing evidence that they help reduce the risk of which other medical issue compared to briefs?

A. Vascular problems
B. Deep vein thrombosis
C. Testicular cancer
D. Hernias

2. Vendors of lingerie in which country are regularly banned for selling the garments?

A. Iran
B. Israel
C. North Korea
D. Sri Lanka

3. Men's sock garters first came into fashion in the which century to hold up the knee-high socks that were popular then?

A. 17th century
B. 18th century
C. 19th century
D. early 20th century

4. Which clothing item was actually considered a piece of men's underwear, and it was impolite to wear them uncovered in polite society for centuries?

A. Socks
B. Suspenders
C. Shirts
D. Waistcoats

5. Contrary to popular belief, men typically despised:

A. Petticoats with large amounts of lace
B. Crinolines/hoop skirts
C. Decorated stockings on women
D. All of the above

DRESSING POLITICALLY

TRUE OR FALSE

1. The British and American suffragists chose to wear white so that they would show up on film well, as early cameras had difficulty with bright colors.
2. Men's trousers that went all the way to the floor rather than ending at the knee only gained popularity during and after the French Revolution, as they had previously only been associated with poor laborers.
3. Mary Tyler Moore was the first woman to wear pants in a sitcom (*The Dick Van Dyke Show*) - on the condition that there was only one scene with her wearing pants per episode.
4. The Black Panther Party adopted the beret as part of their uniform to make them appear more militant.
5. The uniforms of the Nazi party and Hitler Youth were designed by Hugo Boss and manufactured using inmates at forced labor camps.
6. Women began wearing bloomers, or loose, baggy pants, in the 1800s in protest of a ruling by Parliament that decreed they could not own property if they were married.
7. Regency-era women shunned red necklaces and other jewelry because it was too reminiscent of the deaths at the hands of the French Revolution and the guillotine.
8. Homemade clothing in the 1970s saw a resurgence as a means of protesting against consumerism.
9. Those who wished to initially remain out of World War II in the United States took to wearing a red band around their hats or arms.
10. During the Civil Rights Movement of the 1950s and 60s, protestors and activists were told to dress in their Sunday best to look respectable.

MULTIPLE CHOICE

1. The Nazi political soldiers, easy to recognize by their brown shirts, were called what?

A. Righteous Brothers
B. The German Sword
C. Pitiless Ones
D. Stormtroopers

2. The early look of the punk movement, well known for its anti-establishment politics, was designed by Vivien Westwood for which band?

A. Green Day
B. The Sex Pistols
C. The Stooges
D. Black Flag

3. Queen Elizabeth II of England often used which fashion items to show her political standpoint without uttering a word?

A. Jewelry
B. Shoes
C. Hats
D. Purses

4. What did the red cap worn by French Revolutionaries represent?

A. Freedom
B. Brotherhood
C. Liberty
D. The blood of the hated nobility

5. The Rational Dress Society was founded in London to protest restrictive and unnecessary articles of clothing in what year?

A. 1879
B. 1881
C. 1886
D. 1890

SHOES

TRUE OR FALSE

1. The oldest shoes discovered were made from bark in the Pacific Northwest of the United States.
2. The ancient Greeks demanded that everyone wear footwear so that they could be easily distinguished from barefoot slaves.
3. Until 1812, it was illegal for women in Britain to wear boots.
4. Heeled shoes were originally developed for men to help them keep their feet in stirrups better while riding, and also to emphasize their height.
5. Sneakers originated all the way back in the 1870s.
6. It's considered exceptionally rude not to wear shoes indoors in much of Scandinavia.
7. Ötzi, a mummified man found in the Alps, was found with perfectly preserved shoes that were recreated in the 1990s and 2000s.
8. Moccasins were originally intended only for indoor use, to keep feet from tracking dirt inside.
9. Originally, ballet shoes had heels to hold the body in the correct position.
10. Medieval shoes with long toes called *poulaine* were banned at many different times and places because they were so disruptive.

MULTIPLE CHOICE

1. The most expensive sneakers ever sold at auction, a collection of game-worn Micheal Jordans, sold for how many million dollars?

A. Three
B. Eight
C. Six
D. 11

2. In Renaissance Italy, what was the high platform shoe (some even over a foot tall) favored by women of all standings called?

A. Elevante
B. Elegante
C. Chopine
D. Chao-chao

3. In the Old West, cowboys would put their boots into the stirrups of a saddle when they laid down to sleep to prevent what?

A. Scorpions from crawling inside
B. Rain or dirt collecting in them
C. Snakes from curling up to sleep in them
D. Coyotes from stealing them

4. Despite what is commonly shown in TV shows and movies, Vikings did not wear motorcycle boots but shoes made of what?

A. Straw and sheep fur
B. Rawhide
C. Softened leather
D. Twisted reeds and suede

5. While on the space station, what do astronauts typically wear on their feet?

A. Slippers
B. Warm socks
C. Sneakers
D. G-force negating shoes

ACCESSORIES

TRUE OR FALSE

1. There was a special self-defense technique taught to women in the early 1900s that encouraged them to use their enormous hat pins to jab would-be assaulters.
2. It was considered impolite to keep one's gloves on while shaking hands in the 1800s.
3. Men's shirts in the 17th and 18th centuries usually didn't have buttons to hold them closed but were typically held shut at the neck by a cravat wound around the neck and tied in a decorative knot.
4. During the Victorian era, a woman could be arrested under suspicion of being a sex worker simply for not wearing a bonnet and shawl.
5. In the 1940s, women would tie a decorative scarf around their neck in different ways to signal if they were interested in men, women, or both.
6. The first sunglasses were made from melted sea glass and were used to help sailors find the shoreline when the sun made a glare on the ocean.
7. Parasols were used to send secret messages to potential suitors depending on how they were held or twirled.
8. Theodore Roosevelt was the first United States president to wear a modern necktie in an official portrait.
9. Machine-knit socks weren't available until the 1940s when elastic thread was invented.
10. In the 19th and 20th centuries, gloves would sometimes have elaborate decorations printed on them, such as maps, phrases, or little pictures, to act as souvenirs.

MULTIPLE CHOICE

1. Japanese nipple enhancers are not just a fashion trend to make your breasts more noticeable, they also come:

A. In different colors, including glow-in-the-dark
B. In different shapes
C. With pheromone enhancement
D. With sound effects

2. When top hats first entered Western European fashion in the late 1700s, they frequently featured what item around the crown, which usually matched one on the gentleman's shoes?

A. Sash and buckle
B. Ribbon bow
C. Knotted cord
D. Beaded band

3. Spats, cloth, or leather coverings to protect the upper part of shoes, largely fell out of favor for what reason?

A. The King of England stopped wearing them in 1926
B. Returning soldiers from World War I rejected them as reminiscent of their uniforms
C. Materials were in short supply after WWI
D. High-top shoes with fabric uppers replaced them

4. When they first became popular in the 18th century, why didn't gentlemen carry umbrellas?

A. They were a women-only accessory because of their similarity to parasols
B. They would interfere with the traditional sword that most gentlemen carried
C. It was difficult to hold one while riding a horse
D. It could conceal a weapon, and therefore most houses banned them

5. In 16th-century Italy, it was common for civilian men to wear what on their hats in imitation of the military officers at the time?

A. Three colorful bird feathers
B. A badge with a landscape relief
C. Ribbons displaying the colors of their family crest
D. Any of the above.

JEWELRY

TRUE OR FALSE

1. Engagement rings are placed on the third finger of the left hand because it was traditionally used for making oaths in the Roman Empire.
2. Earrings were originally commonly held on with screw backs.
3. The diamond that would eventually become known as the "Hope diamond" originally belonged to Empress Marie Therese of Austria, who gifted it to the future King Louis XVI.
4. Before the inception of watch chains, pocket watches were held up with ribbons, usually richly embroidered with flowers and other patterns.
5. In pre-Columbian South America, *tembetá* are ceremonial lip piercings that were meant to protect the wearer.
6. Engagement rings typically feature diamonds because they are meant to symbolize the bride's purity before her marriage.
7. It was considered taboo for women to be buried wearing necklaces in ancient Egypt, as it would put too much weight on their hearts when they reached the afterlife.
8. Clip-on earrings were invented in the early 20th century.
9. Many ancient Egyptians had their navels pierced, as evident on many statues from the period.
10. Tiaras originated in ancient Iran.

MULTIPLE CHOICE

1. Though piercings have been around since the dawn of human civilization, piercings on which body part are very recent, only originating in the 1970s as part of the punk subculture?

A. Navel
B. Eyebrow
C. Tongue
D. Upper ear

2. A mood ring contains a thermochromic substance made from what substance that changes color based on the temperature applied to it?

A. Plastic
B. Special natural gems
C. Mineral oil
D. Liquid crystal

3. The most expensive purse ever manufactured was 'The Mouawad 1001 Nights Diamond Purse', which was worth... ?

A. $3.8 million
B. $1.25 million
C. $4.3 million
D. $750,000

4. Though they didn't enter the mainstream until the latter half of the 20th century, there is a reference to toe socks (socks with individual 'fingers' for the toes to go into) as far back as when?

A. 1812
B. 1792
C. 1463
D. 1625

5. Lip piercings were common in:

A. Imperial China
B. The Minoan aristocracy
C. Pre-Columbian South America
D. Edo-period Japan

ANSWER KEYS:

Unmentionables

TRUE OR FALSE

1. True
2. False. Corsets were meant to be comfortable for the wearer and act more like a support garment. Tightlacing wasn't even possible until the Industrial Revolution when metal busks and eyelets were available.
3. True
4. True
5. False. Metal wasn't used in foundation garments until the Industrial Revolution. They were meant to be functional, and women did a variety of activities while wearing them, such as household tasks and horseback riding. Most undergarments were stiffened with cords, reeds, or even straw.
6. False. "Bust improvers", which were lightly boned garments that added more shape and volume to the chest, were common in the 1800s. Bust pads were also common to give the desired proportion.
7. True
8. False. Bra-shaped remnants have been found all the way back in the Medieval period, and the women of ancient Greece and Rome used bands of wool to wrap around their chests to support the breasts during exercise.
9. True
10. False. Bullet bras are just one of those quirky fashion things humans have done for seemingly no reason at all.

MULTIPLE CHOICE

1. C
2. A
3. B
4. C
5. B

Dressing Politically

TRUE OR FALSE

1. False. The suffragists were extremely image conscious and chose their appearance with great care. The signature white dresses were chosen to demonstrate their purity symbolically, but also to associate them with middle and upper-class women, as it would take a great deal of work to keep the dresses white.
2. True
3. True
4. False. They adopted it as a symbol of revolution and as homage to Che Guevara.
5. True
6. False. Bloomers were part of the Rational Dress Movement during the mid-1800s and didn't really gain popularity until the later part of the century when women began bicycling and participating in sports more.
7. False. There was actually quite a fad for women to wear red jewels or coral beads around their necks and in earrings as a kind of morbid reference to the guillotine. They would even cut their hair surprisingly short, as everyone had their hair cropped off before going to the guillotine.
8. True
9. False. There was no such fad.
10. True

MULTIPLE CHOICE

1. D
2. B
3. A
4. C
5. B

Shoes

TRUE OR FALSE

1. True
2. False. Shoes were seen as an unnecessary luxury, and nearly everyone went barefoot unless it was physically impossible.
3. False. There has never been any such ban, and women have frequently worn riding and walking boots.
4. True
5. True
6. False. On the contrary, wearing shoes inside private homes is considered exceptionally rude.
7. True
8. False. Moccasins were worn extensively in a variety of climates and were adapted to different terrains.
9. True
10. True

MULTIPLE CHOICE

1. B
2. C
3. A
4. C
5. B

Accessories

TRUE OR FALSE

1. True
2. False. Gloves were to be kept on at nearly all times, except while dining, especially by ladies.
3. True
4. True
5. False. Though there was an increased "blind eye" attitude toward same-sex relationships during the war, there wasn't really a set way of signaling interest via scarves.
6. False. The first sunglasses were made from cut smoky quartz in ancient China.
7. True
8. True
9. False. Knitting machines have existed at least as long as sewing machines, from the 1800s. Machine knit socks were one of the first clothing items available for mass purchase instead of being homemade.
10. True

MULTIPLE CHOICE

1. C
2. A
3. A
4. A
5. B

Jewelry

TRUE OR FALSE

1. False. It was originally thought that the "ring finger" was directly connected to the heart.
2. True
3. False. Marie Theresa never owned the Hope Diamond, although it was owned by Louis XVI before being stolen during the French Revolution.
4. True
5. True
6. False. For many centuries, any stone was acceptable as an engagement ring stone. The fad for using diamonds began in the 20th century.
7. True
8. True
9. False. There is no evidence of navel piercing in ancient Egypt.
10. True

MULTIPLE CHOICE

1. B
2. D
3. A
4. B
5. C

CHAPTER 10:
THE HUMAN BODY

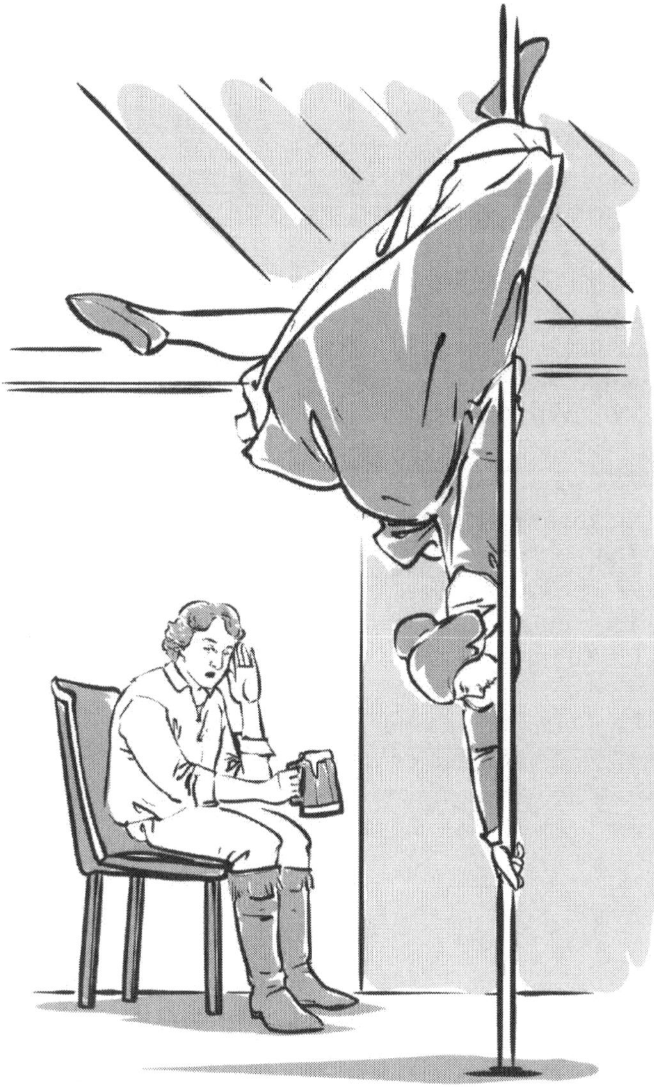

FIVE SENSES

TRUE OR FALSE

1. While the human field of vision is just over 100 degrees wide, the field with actual wide acuity is only two degrees wide.
2. The cells called rods and cones are the only cells in the eye that convert light into electrical impulses for the brain to interpret.
3. The inner part of the ear reaches far into the skull, ending just above the esophagus.
4. The last stage of translating sound from vibrations in the air to electrical impulses is performed by tiny hairs inside the ears' fluid-filled cochlear cavity.
5. The state of tetrachromacy in humans, which allows for seeing a wider range of colors than normal, is a birth defect that eventually causes blindness in old age due to the extra strain placed on the eyes throughout life.
6. The five classical senses as originally described by Aristotle and Gautama Budda are still accepted as the only senses that a human has.
7. The nasal cavity, where the perception of smell is located, is actually slightly larger than the mouth that sits just below it.
8. The sensory receptors are classified into the astroreceptors, metareceptors, cerebroreceptors, and the ossioreceptors.
9. The somatosensory system is the combination of all forms of physical sensation, such as temperature, touch, pain, and the position of all the parts of the body in relation to itself.
10. Though COVID-19 became infamous for disrupting the sense of smell (even permanently), viral infections such as influenza, the common cold, herpes, and hepatitis can also permanently damage the olfactory system to varying degrees.

MULTIPLE CHOICE

1. Smell-training, or actively working to improve or restore the sense of smell, not only helps improve the ability to smell but can also improve:

A. The ability to taste
B. Verbal function
C. Overall well-being
D. All of the above

2. What part of the brain processes visual input?

A. The cerebral cortex
B. The opticus cerberus
C. The encephalic sensorium
D. The cortex visium

3. Loss of hearing has been tied to an increased risk of what, with greater hearing loss increasing the risk?

A. Autism
B. Alzheimer's disease
C. Dyslexia
D. All of the above

4. What is the ability to taste either written or spoken words consistently known as?

A. Auditory-linguistical synesthesia
B. Labial-occlusion synesthesia
C. Lexical-gustatory synesthesia
D. Lingual-gustalitis synesthesia

5. Which is the first sense to develop?

A. Touch
B. Hearing
C. Taste
D. Sight

HEART, BRAIN, LUNGS

TRUE OR FALSE

1. The human heart is roughly the size of a person's hands made into fists and placed together.
2. The diaphragm is one of ten muscles that have equal control of pumping air in and out of human lungs.
3. The cerebral cortex, the part of the brain that is actual gray matter, comprises two layers called the "neocortex" and the "allocortex."
4. Though the spinal cord transmits the signals from the brain to the rest of the body, it is not directly connected to the brain. Instead, the signals are sent through a small chamber filled with neurotransmitter gel, which allows us to turn our head without damaging the connection between the brain and the spinal cord.
5. The human heart is fitted with valves that only allow blood to move in one direction, to prevent backflow.
6. The lung is a complicated organ on the cellular level, evidenced by the fact that 75% of the 20,000 protein-coding genes present in humans are expressed in the cells that make up the lungs.
7. The mucus produced by the lungs is an evolutionary leftover, designed to protect against airborne threats that no longer exist.
8. Aristotle believed the heart to be the seat of intelligence and thought the brain was a cooling mechanism for the blood. He claimed that humans were more rational than animals because of this, as their larger brain cooled their hot-bloodedness more effectively.
9. Memories are stored in one distinct section of the frontal cortex, placing them at risk of loss from external trauma such as hitting your head on the ground.
10. Since 1990, it has been possible to replace a human heart with a completely artificial one, though current-day models are much more sophisticated than the ones available in the 1990s.

MULTIPLE CHOICE

1. Human lungs are divided into lobes, with a total of how many between them?

A. Three
B. Four
C. Five
D. Six

2. When do the lungs finish developing?

A. Before birth
B. In early childhood
C. At the onset of puberty
D. At the end of puberty

3. For an average adult, how many gallons of blood does the heart pump per day?

A. 2,000
B. 1,500
C. 1,000
D. 2,500

4. The brain is made up of what percentage of fat, making it the fattiest organ in the body?

A. 20%
B. 40%
C. 50%
D. 60%

5. What is encephalitis, the inflammation of the brain, typically caused by?

A. Viruses
B. Bacteria
C. Unknown reasons
D. All of the above

REPRODUCTION

TRUE OR FALSE

1. The diagram "Coition of a Hemisected Man and Woman" by Leonardo da Vinci shows a direct line from the woman's uterus to her nipples.
2. For an optimal chance of impregnation, a woman should have sex at least twice per day, as opposed to every one to three days as has previously been recommended.
3. Studies have shown that the position during sex has no relevance for the chance of impregnation, as long as the ejaculation happens in the vagina.
4. The vaginal discharge known as "leukorrhea" is common during pregnancy due to hormonal changes and is usually thin and milky white.
5. In the early stages of pregnancy, the hormonal changes in the woman's body energize her, which is important due to the heightened nest-building instinct that comes with it.
6. The *Kamasutra* is neither exclusively nor predominantly a sex manual on sex positions. Instead, it is a guide for living well, finding partners, maintaining a good sex life, and generally living a life filled with pleasure.
7. Since men don't have an equivalent to the female menopause, the quality of their sperm remains in good condition for their whole lives.
8. The Puritans believed that married couples should have as little sex as possible.
9. Up until the discovery of sperm in 1677, it was believed that prior to fertilization, new humans existed as a tiny version of their adult self within the woman.
10. The clitoris is limited to one central location, and due to its lack of nerve endings, it is mostly irrelevant for a woman's sexual pleasure.

MULTIPLE CHOICE

1. *Mammalian lordosis* is what phenomenon present in most mammalian species, including humans?

A. Male sexual domination
B. Female sexual domination
C. A naturally occurring posture for copulation
D. The process of being "in heat"

2. During pregnancy, the uterus expands up to how many times its original size?

A. 200
B. 500
C. 400
D. 300

3. Wearing what kind of shoes can negatively affect a woman's orgasm because of the pressure it puts on pelvic floor muscles?

A. Flat
B. Wedge heeled
C. High heeled
D. Heavy

4. How long does the average male orgasm last?

A. Six seconds
B. Eight seconds
C. 15 seconds
D. 20 seconds

5. When kissing, people can exchange up to how many bacteria?

A. One million
B. Five million
C. Twenty million
D. One billion

IMMUNE SYSTEM

TRUE OR FALSE

1. While the immune system can distinguish cancer cells, it is limited in its ability to attack and destroy them.
2. Bacteria have no immune systems, leaving them vulnerable to virus infections.
3. There are 80 known autoimmune diseases in humans that cause the body's immune system to attack the body itself.
4. HIV/AIDS is unaffected by the human immune system, despite it increasing exponentially in activity during an HIV infection.
5. Human eyes have their own unique immune system to protect them from infection spreading throughout the rest of the body.
6. The immune system has many layers, activating one at a time in case the previous one has failed to remove the infection.
7. Fingernails are often considered the first defense against disease, acting as a barrier between fingers and surfaces.
8. Because of our appendix, humans are automatically immune to most internal parasites.
9. The skin is the first barrier to protect against infection and is considered a mechanical defense, rather than a chemical or biological one.
10. The immune cells in the bloodstream are called "leukocytes," but are commonly known as "white blood cells."

MULTIPLE CHOICE

1. There's an ounce of truth to the phrase "Laughter is the best medicine," because laughing releases what?

A. Dopamine
B. Serotonin
C. Endorphins
D. All of the above

2. The innate immune system comes pre-loaded with responses to common invasions of the body and is something humans share with what?

A. Plants
B. Fungi
C. Invertebrates
D. All of the above

3. Where does the majority of the immune system originate?

A. Bone marrow
B. The stomach and intestines
C. Tonsils
D. The blood

4. The adaptive immune system has many advantages over the innate, but suffers from what?

A. A limit to how many infections it can store information about
B. A propensity to overreact, causing cytokine storms
C. A delay between exposure and production of relevant antibodies
D. An inability to remember infectious agents long-term

5. Rheumatoid arthritis, an auto-immune disorder, affects which part of the body?

A. Joints
B. Lungs
C. Heart
D. All of the above

SKELETON

TRUE OR FALSE

1. Broken bones are always weaker where they were fractured, which causes many healed fractures to ache long after they're better.
2. The number of bones an adult has continues to diminish as they age due to so many fusing together from conditions such as osteoarthritis in addition to the normal aging process.
3. The functions performed or assisted by the human skeleton are support, movement, endocrine regulation, blood production, protection, and storage of minerals.
4. The bones in feet are technically not connected to one another - this allows the human foot to have such great mobility and flexibility compared to those of other primates.
5. The skeletons of men and women are nearly identical but have differences in the size and shape of the pelvis, canine teeth, skull size, and the long bones of the arms and legs.
6. Bone disease is called "osteopathy," but confusion can occur since this is also the name of an alternative medical practice.
7. The process of first growing a set of baby teeth that are shed to be replaced with larger adult teeth is something humans share with most mammals.
8. Thigh bones, or femurs, are technically slightly curved to allow humans to jump better than our primate ancestors.
9. The oldest human bones discovered were found in Ethiopia and are over 230,000 years old.
10. Bone cancer is a bit of a misnomer, as the cancer doesn't attack the bone itself, but only its ability to produce white blood cells.

MULTIPLE CHOICE

1. Including the wrist, the human hand has how many bones?

A. 27
B. 46
C. 54
D. 38

2. The origin of the word "skeleton" is the ancient Greek *sceletós*. What does it mean?

A. "Dried up"
B. "Frame"
C. "Scaffold"
D. "Bone stand"

3. The smallest and most delicate bone is the stapes, which is located where?

A. Nose
B. Throat
C. Pinky toe
D. Ear

4. What is bone marrow used to store?

A. Iron
B. Oxygen
C. Carbohydrates
D. All of the above

5. What are the joints in the skull that don't allow movement called?

A. Frenulae
B. Sutures
C. Calvarias
D. Osseous indignata

ANSWER KEYS:

Five Senses

TRUE OR FALSE

1. True
2. False. They are joined by photosensitive ganglion cells, to give us complete visual input.
3. False. The inner ear is actually very small.
4. True
5. False. Tetrachromacy is not dangerous and can in fact be beneficial to artists.
6. False. The notion of what is a human sense has expanded significantly since antiquity.
7. True
8. False. They are called chemoreceptors, photoreceptors, mechanoreceptors, thermoreceptors, and nociceptors.
9. True
10. True

MULTIPLE CHOICE

1. D
2. A
3. B
4. C
5. A

Heart, Brain, Lungs

TRUE OR FALSE

1. False. It is roughly the size of one fist.
2. False. Though other muscles can help with breathing, the diaphragm is the main breathing muscle.
3. True
4. False. There is no such thing as neurotransmitter gel in the human body, and the spinal cord does connect to the brain.
5. True
6. True
7. False. Lung mucus is a critical protection system, removing bacteria, viruses, and dust from the airways.
8. True
9. False. Memories are distributed throughout the brain's gray matter. When we wish to recall something, the memories are reassembled like puzzle pieces.
10. True

MULTIPLE CHOICE

1. C
2. B
3. A
4. D
5. D

Reproduction

TRUE OR FALSE

1. True
2. False. Sex every one to three days is generally enough for impregnation.
3. True
4. True
5. False. The hormonal changes are very tiring, making assistance from family with everyday things very helpful.
6. True
7. False. Sperm quality degrades as a man grows older, as well as
8. decreasing in quantity.
9. False. The Puritans actually allowed divorce on the grounds of a woman not being sexually satisfied by her husband.
10. True
11. False. The clitoris extends along the length of the vagina, as well as around it. It also has more nerve endings than any other part of a woman's anatomy.

MULTIPLE CHOICE

1. C
2. B
3. C
4. A
5. D

Immune system

TRUE OR FALSE

1. True
2. False. Bacteria have a very basic defense against viruses based on enzymes.
3. True
4. False. HIV/AIDS specifically targets the human immune system, greatly weakening it.
5. False. The eyes use the same immune system as all the other parts of the body.
6. True
7. False. The fingernails do protect the fingertip from some injuries, however.
8. False. The appendix does not protect from internal parasites, but it has been suggested it acts as a reservoir for friendly gut bacteria.
9. True
10. True

MULTIPLE CHOICE

1. A
2. D
3. B
4. C
5. D

Skeleton

TRUE OR FALSE

1. False. The bone actually becomes stronger in that spot.
2. False. Once adulthood is reached, humans do not lose any more bones.
3. True
4. False. All bones are connected in some fashion, otherwise the skeleton wouldn't function properly.
5. True
6. True
7. True
8. False. Femurs are completely straight.
9. True
10. False. Bone cancer aggressively attacks bones, which can be seen on skeletons long after death.

MULTIPLE CHOICE

1. C
2. A
3. D
4. A
5. B

CHAPTER 11:
NATURE

FUNGI

TRUE OR FALSE

1. *Cordyceps* mushrooms are parasitic, mostly preying on insects but also other mushrooms.
2. Mushrooms that grow in soil prefer to grow far from trees, since trees have bigger roots that absorb the nutrients they are both competing for much more efficiently.
3. The tastiest mushrooms are also the most poisonous, requiring special preparation by a master chef to be safe to eat.
4. Though animals large and small - from scavengers to insects and even bacteria, are important - fungi are the main decomposers in every ecosystem.
5. Mushrooms are a recent evolutionary development, having come into existence shortly after the extinction event that wiped out the dinosaurs.
6. Distinct species of fungus can reproduce in more ways than one, including both sexual and asexual reproduction in the same species.
7. Many types of mushrooms are used in traditional folk medicine all over the world but are especially prominent in traditional Chinese medicine.
8. The radiation from nuclear disasters, such as in Chornobyl, kills off all types of fungi, causing the decomposition of dead plants and animals in the region to stop completely.
9. Whether a mold or a mushroom, fungi need very specific conditions in order to survive.
10. Penicillin, the world's first antibiotic, is cultivated from a mold.

MULTIPLE CHOICE

1. Traditional fungicidal treatments across the world include:

A. Jojoba oil, rosemary oil, and the bacteria *Bacillus subtilis*
B. Saltwater on affected organisms such as animals or crops
C. Cutting out and burning the affected area
D. All of the above

2. What is foot fungus, also called "athlete's foot," spread via?

A. Water
B. Through the air
C. Direct and indirect contact, like towels or locker room floors
D. Walking barefoot outside

3. Truffles, a delicacy spread around the world, are first mentioned in what century?

A. 16th century BCE
B. 20th century BCE
C. 1st century BCE
D. 4th century CE

4. Like other eukaryotic cells, fungi have what?

A. A membrane-enclosed nucleus
B. Flagella
C. Extremophiles
D. Methanogens

5. What is the study of fossil fungi called?

A. Herbocology
B. Paleomycelia
C. Paleomycology
D. Archeopathology

ANIMAL KINGDOM

TRUE OR FALSE

1. Crocodile teeth are very securely fastened in their jaws, more so than most predators, ensuring that they don't lose any of their teeth while performing the infamous death roll after grabbing prey with their mouth.
2. Horses are among the few creatures that evolved to have a single toe (hoof) from the beginning.
3. Animals are defined by belonging to the *animalia kingdom* by virtue of being eukaryotic organisms with multiple cells, as opposed to the single-cell bacteria.
4. Vertebrae animals began to move on to land in the Devonian period, around 390 million years ago, but arthropods like crustaceans, centipedes, and later, insects and spiders, won the race to land by a 30-million-year stretch.
5. Penguins can communicate via echolocation like many other aquatic animals.
6. The bull shark is known for leaving the warm ocean around Australia and Brazil, where it normally lives, and swimming upstream in freshwater rivers, sometimes going as far as Illinois, 700 miles from the ocean.
7. Tarantulas have been known to form cooperative colonies to hunt larger prey, especially during egg-laying season.
8. Solitary bees don't live alone and do form hives. However, there is no division of labor and since every female is producing eggs, there is no queen.
9. Unlike their cousins the tiger, there are no known lions that will voluntarily swim.
10. To determine the age of a blue whale, all you need to do is count the rings in its waxy ear plug, just like the rings of a tree.

MULTIPLE CHOICE

1. Placoderms, from the Greek words for plate and skin, are an extinct form of which creature?

A. A prehistoric crocodile
B. Fish with armored heads
C. Lizards with unusually thick skin for their size
D. Armored flightless birds

2. In elephant herds, when the matriarch dies or is no longer fit to be matriarch, who is she replaced by?

A. The matriarch's sister
B. The strongest female in the herd
C. The matriarch's oldest daughter
D. None of the above

3. Though commonly known as a saber-tooth tiger, it is not actually a tiger. What is its proper scientific name?

A. Smilodon
B. Felidae gracilias
C. Dentadon
D. Felidon

4. Though the octopus as we know it today has only experienced one extinction event, the family of cephalopods to which they belong have made it through how many of them?

A. Two
B. Three
C. Four
D. Five

5. The black panther is not a single species of big cat, but a melanistic what?

A. Lion
B. Jaguar
C. Leopard
D. B and C

OCEANS

TRUE OR FALSE

1. The ocean covers 70.8% of the world's surface and contains 97% of its water.
2. At a depth of 219 yards, only 1% of the sunlight at the surface is visible in the ocean.
3. The continental shelf is where one continental plate sinks underneath another.
4. The water circulations that create the currents are created by variations in saltiness, temperature, and wind.
5. The ocean contains just under two million known species.
6. The various depth zones of the ocean are called the Epipelagic, Mesopelagic, Bathypelagic, Abyssalpelagic, and Hadalpelagic zones.
7. The total volume of the water in the ocean is 431,003,331 cubic miles.
8. Sea ice contains high amounts of salt.
9. The ocean is divided into five sections: the Atlantic, Pacific, Indian, Arctic, and Antarctic oceans.
10. All the planets in the solar system affect the Earth's tides.

MULTIPLE CHOICE

1. What were the green oceans during the Permian-Triassic extinction event caused by?

A. Algae blooming
B. Sulfur-eating bacteria
C. Seaweeds not getting eaten due to fish dying off
D. Plankton

2. The White Shark Café is a place where great white sharks gather every year for reasons currently unknown. Where is it located?

A. North Atlantic Ocean
B. Antarctic Sea
C. Pacific Ocean
D. South China Sea

3. The deepest part of the Mariana Trench, the Challenger Deep, is approximately how many feet deep?

A. 35,000
B. 30,000
C. 41,000
D. 29,000

4. One milliliter of ocean water can contain up to how many viruses?

A. 500,000
B. 12 million
C. Ten million
D. One million

5. Crabs with fur-lined pincers, or *kiwa*, are known as what?

A. Yeti crabs
B. Stubble crabs
C. Maned crabs
D. Pompom crabs

BOTANICAL ODDITIES

TRUE OR FALSE

1. Giant water lily pads can hold a child without sinking.
2. The bleeding-heart plant gets its name from the blood-red nectar that drips from the heart-shaped plant in the morning.
3. Japanese blood grass is commonly used to create a barrier between a garden and the wild in areas prone to wildfires since it is naturally flame-resistant.
4. The plant known as 'strangle weed' and 'witches' hair' lacks chlorophyll for photosynthesis and instead feeds on other plants to get the nutrients it needs.
5. In the practice of sending messages through flower arrangements, a common occurrence in Victorian England, Basil was used to express tender feelings that were not outright love.
6. The berries from the belladonna plant are very nutritious, in addition to being delicious.
7. The shape of the 9.8-feet tall and foul-smelling flower of the *Amorphophallus Titanum* plant is the cause of its name, which means "giant misshapen penis."
8. The flower of the cockscomb plant resembles a brain and is known to cause sleepiness if eaten.
9. The White Baneberry is also known as "Doll's Eyes," due to the small black dot on the berries. This makes the plant look like it is growing clusters of eyes.
10. While some species of fungi are parasitic on plants, the ghost flower, which gets its name from its white chlorophyll-less body, is parasitic on various types of fungus.

MULTIPLE CHOICE

1. *Nepenthes lowii* is the only plant in the world that evolved to do what?

A. Collect and feed off animal droppings
B. Move independently
C. Move underground during inclement weather
D. Respond to touch

2. Where do carnivorous plants generate their energy from?

A. Consuming prey in the form of bugs or small animals
B. Nutrients taken up through their roots
C. Photosynthesis via chlorophyll
D. All of the above

3. *Lithops*, or "living stones" as they are sometimes known, are actually what?

A. Succulents
B. A form of lichen
C. Cacti
D. None of the above

4. The black bat flower is a member of the which family, despite it not producing edible fruit?

A. Melon
B. Yam
C. Nightshade
D. Carrot

5. The fairy lantern is only visible when it flowers. Where does it get its nourishment from?

A. Absorbing nutrients via an extensive root system
B. Allow burrowing insects to live inside it and feeding on them when they die
C. Underground fungi
D. Living parasitically on tree roots

DESERTS AND JUNGLES

TRUE OR FALSE

1. Deserts are not classified by the amount of sand or the temperature in an area but by the amount of rainfall. This is why both the Arctic and Antarctic regions of Earth are considered deserts.
2. The word "jungle" came to English from the Hindustani word for forest.
3. During the height of the last ice age, the cooler temperatures allowed for more rain in what is now the Sahara Desert, causing it to be covered in rainforest.
4. Deserts are increasingly seen as sources of potential solar energy, with vast installations currently built in the Mojave desert.
5. While jungles have a diverse flora and fauna, clear similarities can be seen all over the world, making classification of the various species a simple matter.
6. The Gobi Desert was the source of the first dinosaur eggs and remains a rich source of various fossils.
7. Another word for jungle is rainforest, since the daily rain promotes the wild growth of the plants.
8. The ice covering the Antarctic Desert is relatively thin, since the lack of rain and snow in the area has not allowed for any significant glacial formation.
9. While humans have likely waged war in desert areas as long as humans have lived there, the historical record of specific desert conflicts only stretch back to the Muslim-Quraysh War between 624 and 630 CE.
10. The El Yunque National Forest in Northern Puerto Rico is the only tropical jungle to be under the care of the European Union.

MULTIPLE CHOICE

1. The Gobi Desert expands by 1390 square miles every year, damaging the agriculture of which country?

A. Mongolia
B. China
C. Siberia
D. Turkmenistan

2. Lake Vostok may be the largest subglacial lake in Antarctica, but the cold desert continent has how many known subglacial lakes?

A. Seven
B. 42
C. 421
D. 675

3. The desert region covering northern Mexico and parts of the southwestern United States is called what?

A. Chihuahua Desert
B. Texico Desert
C. Arimexian Desert
D. The Dry Flats

4. The term rainforest began to replace the misnomer "jungle" in the:

A. 1910s
B. 1970s
C. 1980s
D. 1940s

5. What continent has the greatest amount of forest cover?

A. South America
B. Asia
C. Africa
D. Europe

ANSWER KEYS:

Fungi

TRUE OR FALSE

1. True
2. False. Many mushrooms live in symbiosis with trees, trading resources with each other.
3. False. Unlike the fish *fugu*, you can't fix poison mushrooms.
4. True
5. False. Fungi have been around for at least 460 million years.
6. True
7. True
8. False. Some mushrooms have specialized to feed off the nuclear radiation.
9. False. Fungi are quite sturdy, and some can even survive space travel.
10. True

MULTIPLE CHOICE

1. A
2. C
3. B
4. A
5. C

Animal Kingdom

TRUE OR FALSE

1. False. Crocodiles can regrow each tooth 50 times.
2. False. The ancestors of horses had five toes, that over time became just a single one. Remnants of these extra toes can sometimes be seen on the inside of horses' legs.
3. True
4. True
5. False. Penguins have no echo location at all.
6. True
7. False. Tarantulas are solitary predators.
8. True
9. False. Okavango lions are great swimmers and spend a lot of time in the water during flood season.
10. True

MULTIPLE CHOICE

1. B
2. C
3. A
4. D
5. D

Oceans

TRUE OR FALSE

1. True
2. True
3. False. The continental shelf is the shallow part of the ocean where dry land slowly transitions into the deep ocean.
4. True
5. False. Only 230,000 known species live in the ocean, but about 2,000,000 are suspected to live there still undiscovered.
6. True
7. False. It is only 321,003,271 cubic miles.
8. False. While sea ice does contain some salt, it is much less than the water around it.
9. True
10. False. Only the moon is close enough to affect the Earth's tides.

MULTIPLE CHOICE

1. B
2. C
3. A
4. C
5. A

Botanical Oddities

TRUE OR FALSE

1. True
2. False. It just looks like a heart. No nectar, blood-colored or otherwise, drips from it.
3. False. It is no less flammable than any other grass, but it burns at higher temperatures, increasing the risk of spreading a wildfire.
4. True
5. False. Basil symbolized hatred.
6. False. Belladonna is also known as "deadly nightshade," and for good reason, as the berries cause hallucinations and eventually death.
7. True
8. False. While it does resemble a brain, it does not cause sleepiness. It is, however, used for food and soap making in western Africa.
9. True
10. True

MULTIPLE CHOICE

1. A
2. C
3. A
4. B
5. C

Deserts and Jungles

TRUE OR FALSE

1. True
2. True
3. False. While the Sahara Desert does grow and shrink in cycles of thousands of years, during the ice age it was actually larger than it is today.
4. True
5. False. Jungles grow over many different climate zones and elevations, causing each one to be highly unique in terms of weather, plants, and animals.
6. True
7. False. The dense forestation of jungles is common on the edges of rainforests where there is more sunlight, but jungles can and do grow in other areas, not just rainy ones.
8. False. Not only does Antarctica hold 70% of the world's fresh water in its glaciers, were it to melt, the sea levels would rise by 66 yards worldwide.
9. True
10. False. It is under the care of the United States Forest Service.

MULTIPLE CHOICE

1. B
2. D
3. A
4. B
5. D

CHAPTER 12:
SCIENCE

SPACE

TRUE OR FALSE

1. The baseline temperature in space is 2.7 kelvin, equivalent to -455 degrees Fahrenheit. This places the temperature just above absolute zero, the lowest temperature possible.
2. Since Mars currently lacks a magnetic field to protect its atmosphere from being blown away by the solar wind, in 2017 it was proposed to place a magnetic field generator in a distant orbit between the Sun and Mars. This would create an artificial field to protect Mars, allowing the planet to rebuild its atmosphere.
3. Black holes get their names from their ability to trap light in their gravity field but still allowing other forms of electromagnetic radiation to escape. This is because light is also a particle.
4. The gravity well of a planet or star is called so because it is the source of gravity, much like a regular well is a water source.
5. Space weather is the influence the Sun, and the heliosphere generally, has on primarily Earth and its magnetosphere, but also on other planets in the solar system.
6. When suddenly exposed to a vacuum, such as if all the air in a space vehicle were sucked out through a puncture in the hull, the human body quickly swells up and explodes.
7. Dark matter is called such, due to how it absorbs all visible light being directed at it, while reflecting other forms of electromagnetic radiation such as radio waves and X-rays.
8. Based on the *Lithopanspermia hypothesis*, it has been suggested that rocks carrying bacteria, or even simpler building blocks of life, may have been ejected from Earth, Mars, and Venus by meteor impacts and thrown in the direction of the neighboring planets, scattering life between them in the solar system's early days.
9. While it would be possible to simulate gravity in outer space through the use of a rotating spaceship or space station, it would not only be cost-prohibitive to build due to the size, but it is also possible that the rotation would cause inner ear destabilization of the occupants, causing nausea and disorientation.
10. TRAPPIST-1 is a red dwarf star only 40 light years from Earth with seven known planets, all gas giants.

MULTIPLE CHOICE

1. The Pioneer 10 space probe was the first spacecraft to reach escape velocity from the solar system at its launch in 1972. It was, however, overtaken by which faster space probe in 2023?

A. Explorer 7
B. Discovery 3
C. Voyager 2
D. Enterprise C

2. The James Webb Telescope is the largest space telescope in the solar system as of 2024. It is designed to view the universe in which section of the electromagnetic spectrum?

A. Infrared
B. Visible
C. Ultraviolet
D. Radio

3. The comet Shoemaker-Levy 9 was unique in that it orbited which planet rather than the Sun, which it would collide with in 2009?

A. Neptune
B. Jupiter
C. Uranus
D. Saturn

4. What is the name of the point in the Heliosphere where the solar wind weakens to the point that it is no longer able to push away the gas of the interstellar medium of outer space?

A. Interstellar pushback
B. Helios Disruptus
C. Void bubble
D. Termination shock

5. Which distant dwarf planet is tied with Ceres in the asteroid belt as the largest dwarf planet that does not have a moon?

A. Mercury
B. Sedna
C. Pluto
D. Ganymede

BIOLOGY

TRUE OR FALSE

1. Cells get their name from the cellulose structure of plants where they were first discovered in 1736.
2. While it was originally believed that the epigenetic mechanisms that control what part of an organism's DNA is expressed are reset at reproduction, it has been shown that some of it does carry over, allowing the offspring to express genetic traits the parents could not use.
3. There is a fossil of a single-cell organism that shows the existence of LUCA, or "Last Universal Common Ancestor," from which all the domains of life descend.
4. The presence of large amounts of oxygen in the oceans and atmosphere of the young Earth was essential for the formation of the first life forms.
5. The algae *Valonia ventricosa*, also known as "sailor's eyeball" or "sea grape," is a single-cell organism that is between 0.39 and 1.57 inches wide.
6. Sexual reproduction predates multicellular organisms by approximately 400 million years.
7. There are 1,300 different species of tardigrades, all of which are extremely resilient, capable of surviving nuclear radiation, starvation, dehydration, vacuum, extreme temperature, and even deep space.
8. The platypus is the only mammal that survived into the current age that lays eggs.
9. The order of taxonomy that defines an organism's place in the tree of life is Domain, Kingdom, Phylum, Class, Order, Family, Genus, and Species.
10. A single member of the tree species Wollemi Pine has successfully cloned itself for at least 60 million years, making it the oldest living multicell organism in the world, since each new plant is identical to each of its forebears.

MULTIPLE CHOICE

1. Amino acids are part of the construction of DNA, and together the many different kinds build various what?

A. Proteins
B. Fats
C. Carbohydrates
D. All of the above

2. Chitin is found in the cell walls of fungi and the exoskeletons of all arthropods. What is it?

A. A bio ceramic
B. A polymer
C. An alloy
D. A peptide

3. Bioluminescence is caused by the blending of a light-emitting molecule and an enzyme. What are they called?

A. Lampsi and fosiferia
B. Lucifer and glowium
C. Luxuria and lucium
D. Luciferin and luciferase

4. Part of the reason why a gecko can climb on any surface except Teflon is the:

A. Presence of millions of hairlike setae on their feet
B. Hundreds of tiny suction cups
C. Sharpness of their claws
D. B and C

5. While rats are often blamed for the spread of disease, the bubonic plague was actually transmitted by what?

A. Fleas
B. Birds
C. Poor sanitation
D. Trick question – it was the rats, actually

METEOROLOGY

TRUE OR FALSE

1. A storm is any continuous amount of wind reaching or surpassing at least a rating ten on the Beaufort Scale, at least 55 mph. The presence of lightning and thunder has no connection to it, even though it is commonly called a thunderstorm.
2. Weather has been studied in great detail for most of human history, with reasonably accurate predictions going back to at least 2300 BCE.
3. The launch of the first weather satellite TIROS-1 in 1960 marked the beginning of globally gathered weather information.
4. While the announcers of weather forecasts are often considered meteorologists, few of them actually are. Instead, they are reporters with varying degrees of education on weather phenomena.
5. The study of the "Boundary Layer" in meteorology concerns itself with the weather patterns at the outer edge of Earth's atmosphere.
6. With the rise in computer simulation for weather prediction, the lack of accurate reports is increasingly due to human error in entering and interpreting weather data.
7. The towering portion of a thundercloud is largely an optical illusion caused by the buildup of electric charge in the cloud warping the air.
8. By the standard of meteorologists, winter is considered to be the three consecutive months with the lowest temperature.
9. In the United States, February 5 is National Weatherperson Day, celebrating the contribution of meteorologists and weather reporters everywhere.
10. Mist and fog, due to their high humidity, are considered to be precipitation, similar to rain and snow.

MULTIPLE CHOICE

1. During Black Sunday, a particularly violent dust storm during the Dust Bowl, it's estimated that how many tons of topsoil were displaced?

A. 100,000
B. 75,000
C. 25,000
D. 300,000

2. In a tornado, where are the strongest winds?

A. At ground level
B. Higher in the atmosphere
C. In the middle, where the rotation is strongest
D. Just above the tornado

3. For a hurricane to form, the ocean water temperature must be at or above how many degrees Fahrenheit?

A. 65
B. 79
C. 72
D. 69

4. For severe and dangerous weather to spawn there has to be what?

A. High temperatures
B. Moisture
C. Atmospheric instability
D. All of the above

5. An average cloud 0.39 square miles in size weighs...?

A. 1,500 pounds
B. 500,000 pounds
C. 1.1 million pounds
D. 756,000 pounds

AI/ROBOTICS

TRUE OR FALSE

1. Thanks to the advancements in both hardware and software, as of March 2024, an AI system can think independently for itself, if only in a very rudimentary manner.
2. AI systems are quite energy efficient thanks to their ability to regulate their own power usage.
3. Robotics crossed the line into medicine in 1994 with the creation of the first mechanical prosthetic hand that had a sense of touch.
4. Electroactive polymers are a type of plastic that contracts or expands based on electric stimulation, effectively making it artificial muscles that can be used by robots to move more like a human does.
5. The first self-learning computer program was created in 1955 and was able to teach itself to play checkers better the more it played.
6. Though they are not yet very advanced or widespread, there are self-operating ground-based weapon platforms - combat robots by another name - that can select and neutralize targets without human input.
7. The play *R.U.R.* or *Rossum's Universal Robots* by Austria-Hungarian playwright Karel Čapek, had its English premiere in 1923, introducing the word "robot" to the English language.
8. The ethical questions of using AI are numerous and complicated, including copyright and effective art theft, making human labor obsolete, and the spread of false and biased information, to mention just a few.
9. The CAPTCHA test was developed in 1997 and is based on Alan Turing's theories about how to prove that a request to a computer system comes from a human and not another computer.
10. The science fiction idea of a positronic brain as the computer of a robot is being actively researched as a possible avenue for creating robots that can think.

MULTIPLE CHOICE

1. While still in the very early stage of research and development, it is thought that nanorobotics will first see use in which field?

A. Space exploration
B. Medicine
C. The military
D. Heavy industry

2. Though functional robots and AI have come about in the past 100 years, humans have dreamed about creating artificial life since at least what year, when the first written records of such things emerged?

A. 1764
B. 1400 BCE
C. 50 CE
D. 600 BCE

3. What is the name of the first (and so far, only) flying robot sent to Mars?

A. Ingenuity, nicknamed Ginny
B. Adventurer, nicknamed Advent
C. Ranger, nicknamed Reggi
D. Discoverer, nicknamed Disco

4. Artificial General Intelligence is the goal of current AI research. As of 2023, how many AGI research projects are there across how many nations?

A. 41 projects in 26 nations
B. 57 projects in 48 nations
C. 72 projects in 37 nations
D. 98 projects in 64 nations

5. In medicine, AI can be used to provide what faster than humans can?

A. Diagnoses
B. Treatment
C. Prevention plans
D. All of the above

GEOLOGY

TRUE OR FALSE

1. The Mid-Atlantic Ridge is an underwater volcanic mountain range that runs along the Atlantic from north to south.
2. The temperature of lava is what determines the speed at which it flows.
3. Just before an earthquake, it is possible to see glowing in the air above the site of the tectonic stress that is similar to northern lights.
4. Five of the 16 tectonic plates that make up the Earth's crust have no land above sea level.
5. All lava is red or orange when it first comes out of the volcano.
6. The only way to exactly date a geological formation is to cut it apart, or take a drill sample, and measure the thickness and number of the layers in the formation.
7. A lava tube, also called a pyroduct, forms when lava of one mineral type hardens on top of a different kind of lava, creating a long enclosed space.
8. Thanks to early detection systems for volcanic activity, scientists can not only predict when and where an eruption will take place, but in some cases can send a team of geo-engineers to drill into the tunnels that feed lava to the volcano and release the pressure, so the eruption is prevented.
9. The walls of the Grand Canyon, and the many caves within them, have been used for human habitation by Native Americans in the area for thousands of years.
10. The high value of diamonds is due to their rarity.

MULTIPLE CHOICE

1. The speed and spin direction of the Earth's solid metal core changes over the course of how many years?

A. 113
B. 70
C. 59
D. 40

2. During the nine-year-long eruption of the Parícutin volcano in Mexico, which movie took advantage and used the eruption as backdrop scenery?

A. *Garden of Evil*
B. *The Devil's Breath*
C. *El Dorado*
D. *Captain from Castille*

3. The San Francisco Earthquake in 1906 was so strong that it caused surface displacement of how many feet?

A. 15
B. 12
C. 25
D. 20

4. Studying the weather and climate of the distant past through examination of rock sediments using core samples and cliff shears, is a geological discipline called what?

A. Paleoclimatology
B. Geopetraology
C. Hydropaleology
D. Climapetraology

5. The state of California has over how many seismic faults, with more being continually discovered?

A. 500
B. 1,200
C. 7,800
D. 15,700

ANSWER KEYS:

Space

TRUE OR FALSE

1. True
2. True
3. False. Nothing can escape a black hole. The radiation we can observe from black holes is generated just outside the point of no return.
4. False. The gravity well is the sphere of influence around an object in space, often illustrated as a flat surface with a pit in the middle to show the influence that the object has.
5. True
6. False. This is a persistent myth. What does happen is that with the loss of pressure, the water in the body is able to boil at normal body temperature. This causes the water to quickly vaporize and expand, rupturing the lungs, bursting blood vessels, and bloating the body.
7. False. Dark matter does not interact with electromagnetic radiation at all and can only be detected by the effects of its gravity on objects around it.
8. True
9. True
10. False. A full four of TRAPPIST-1's planets are confirmed to be rocky, one of which is just barely larger than Earth.

MULTIPLE CHOICE

1. C
2. A
3. B
4. D
5. B

Biology

TRUE OR FALSE

1. False. They were discovered in 1665 by Robert Hooke. He named them cells from the Latin word *cellula*, meaning "little room," because he thought they resembled the cells that monks inhabit as their private quarters.
2. True
3. False. There is no fossil of L.U.C.A.; its existence is inferred by the similarities of the cellular structure of all current life, regardless of the domain to which it belongs.
4. False. Oxygen was originally a waste product from cyanobacteria, the first organisms to develop photosynthesis.
5. True
6. True
7. True
8. False. The four different species of echidna, close biological relatives of the platypus, also lay eggs.
9. True
10. True

MULTIPLE CHOICE

1. A
2. B
3. D
4. A
5. A

Meteorology

TRUE OR FALSE

1. True
2. False. While weather prediction has been a part of human culture for all of recorded history, and probably before, up until the 18th century it relied primarily on historical knowledge and religion.
3. True
4. True
5. False. It is actually about the weather and atmosphere close to the ground.
6. False. The massive computational power needed, combined with the inherently chaotic nature of the atmosphere, makes weather prediction unreliable no matter how good the information provided to the computer is.
7. False. Thunderclouds rise from close to the ground level to very high altitudes.
8. True
9. True
10. False. Because mist and fog do not condense into water drops that fall to the ground, they are not precipitation. They are much more like a very low-to-the-ground cloud than anything else.

MULTIPLE CHOICE

1. D
2. A
3. B
4. D
5. C

AI/Robotics

TRUE OR FALSE

1. False. As of March 2024, computers are still not able to think for themselves, relying on human-made input, and are only able to recognize and replicate patterns.
2. False. AIs are excessively hungry for energy, and training even the simplest AI can produce over 600,000 pounds of carbon dioxide.
3. False. It was not until 2009 that the first robotic hand for human prosthetic use was created that could transmit a sense of touch. Fifteen years later, the sensation is still very limited compared to an actual human hand.
4. True
5. True
6. False. These systems do not exist yet, and all have a human remote controlling them, ensuring that ethics have a chance to enter the decision-making process before firing a weapon.
7. True
8. True
9. True
10. False. Positrons, being antimatter, would convert themselves and their corresponding electron into energy at the moment they make contact.

MULTIPLE CHOICE

1. B
2. D
3. A
4. C
5. D

Geology

TRUE OR FALSE

1. True
2. False. The mineral composition of lava, as well as the incline, also determines the flow speed.
3. True
4. True
5. False. The Ol Doinyo Lengai volcano in Africa has totally black lava.
6. False. Measuring the amount of different radioactive isotopes and cross-referencing the results is the method used by geologists when an exact dating is needed.
7. True
8. False. There is no way of preventing a volcanic eruption.
9. True
10. False. Diamonds are actually quite common, and their value is greatly inflated. Painite is the rarest type of gemstone in the world, with just over 1,000 found.

MULTIPLE CHOICE

1. B
2. D
3. D
4. A
5. D

CHAPTER 13:
MODERN HISTORY

PROHIBITION

TRUE OR FALSE

1. Temperance as a societal concept originated with the Puritans.
2. It is estimated that by 1925 there were anywhere between 30,000 and 100,000 speakeasies in New York City alone.
3. Bootleg jeans are so named because bootleggers would hide flasks of alcohol tied to their calves so they could transport them unseen.
4. During the early to mid-20th century, most support for Prohibition came from Protestant denominations in the Southern United States.
5. Woodrow Wilson was a staunch supporter of Prohibition and refused to have alcohol in the White House.
6. It was illegal to consume alcohol, and anyone caught doing so would face fines and likely jail time.
7. To combat people using ethyl alcohol to make alcoholic drinks, the federal government ordered more and more dangerous poisons to be added to it.
8. Prohibition enforcement was usually targeted at the rich, who had the means to buy bootleg alcohol at exorbitant prices.
9. It was common for clergymen to form vigilante groups to combat bootleggers and smugglers since the official authorities lacked both the numbers and organization to effectively enforce Prohibition.
10. The KKK were vehemently opposed to bootlegging and threatened to denounce or even take direct action against bootleggers.

MULTIPLE CHOICE

1. After serving his sentence for tax evasion, Al Capone became one of the first Americans to do what?

A. Own a color television
B. Be treated with penicillin for advanced syphilis
C. File a lawsuit against the US government
D. Recoup some of his money from the IRS

2. Which state was the last state to repeal Prohibition in 1966, though it does still have many dry counties?

A. Utah
B. Ohio
C. Oregon
D. Mississippi

3. Speakeasies were also known as what?

A. Blind pigs
B. Hooch dens
C. Countertops
D. Stoolies

4. Which state never bothered to enforce Prohibition, even though it was illegal to produce, transport, and sell alcohol there?

A. Texas
B. Oklahoma
C. Maryland
D. Florida

5. Prohibitionists actually formed a political party, and much like the Democrats and the Republicans, they too picked an animal to be their mascot. Which animal did they choose?

A. Camel
B. Pig
C. Eagle
D. Whale

THE SPACE RACE

TRUE OR FALSE

1. Before World War I, there was a push for Britain to attempt to ballistically launch a capsule at the moon with a man inside so that he could claim the moon for the British Empire.
2. The space race arose as an extension to the ballistic missile arms race between the Soviet Union and the United States.
3. The United States rejected the help of scientists who could be proven to be certified members of the Nazi party, fearing their loyalty was suspect.
4. The United States had a thriving rocket research program through the 1920s and 30s, headed by Robert H. Goddard.
5. The classical space station of 1950s science fiction was based on the space station concept created by Werner von Braun as part of the United States' efforts to win the space race.
6. The rocket that launched *Sputnik 1*, humanity's first artificial satellite, was not designed specifically for that kind of mission as it was an intercontinental ballistic missile.
7. The Soviet Union and the United States had a strict policy of avoiding each other in outer space until the 1990s after the USSR fell.
8. The Soviet Union was the first to hit many milestones in the space race, having not only the first satellite, but also the first man, the first spacewalk, and the first woman in space.
9. Buzz Aldrin, the second man on the moon, was the first astronaut from the United States to have a doctoral degree.
10. The moon landing, seen as the victory point of the space race, was vehemently disputed by the Soviet Union as a fake for many years.

MULTIPLE CHOICE

1. During the Apollo 11 mission that landed the first humans on the moon, at which point did astronauts Neil Armstrong and Buzz Aldrin have the highest heart rates?

A. During take-off
B. Landing in the *Eagle* lunar lander
C. While exiting the *Eagle*
D. When planting the American flag

2. The *Saturn V* rocket used in the first manned moon mission was multistage. How many stages were there?

A. Three
B. Four
C. Five
D. Six

3. During the first American spacewalk, from the *Gemini IV* mission, which of the following happened:

A. A defect in the hatch nearly cost the astronauts their lives
B. An umbilical line was used to feed oxygen to the spacesuit
C. A hand-held maneuvering device was used
D. All of the above

4. During the first EVA, or Extra Vehicular Activity, in 1965, Soviet cosmonaut Alexi Leonov got stuck in the exterior airlock hatch for how many minutes when returning to his spacecraft?

A. 30
B. 10
C. 12
D. 18

5. The Space Race, and indeed any form of rocket-propelled activity, wouldn't have been possible without the rocketry equation created by who in which year?

A. Robert Goddard in 1935
B. Konstantin Tsiolkovsky in 1903
C. Hermann Oberth in 1921
D. William Coleman in 1934

ASSASSINATIONS, COUPS, AND PLOTS

TRUE OR FALSE

1. In an attempt to find the people responsible for government leaks, John F. Kennedy had the CIA wiretap the communications of journalists in an operation called Project Mockingbird.
2. John Wilkes Booth, the man who assassinated Abraham Lincoln, was identified after his death at the hands of pursuing soldiers partly by a tattoo on his left hand.
3. In 1961 and 1962, only six months apart, two KGB officers defected to the United States. Both accused the other of being a double agent, and the spread of suspicion ended the careers of many CIA agents. To this day, the truth or lies of their claims is still not fully understood.
4. Robert F. Kennedy's security team is credited with finding and subduing his assassin, Sirhan Sirhan, in the immediate aftermath.
5. Though many plots were floated as possibilities, the CIA never actually attempted to assassinate Fidel Castro.
6. There was a plot ready to be executed by the United States intelligence community to frame Stalin as a dedicated Satanist as a means of discrediting him to the Soviet people. He died before it could be enacted.
7. In the aftermath of the death of Mao Zedong, a group known as the Gang of Four attempted to overthrow the government of the People's Republic of China.
8. Despite many conspiracies, the United States government has never been found to be responsible in any way for the assassination of Martin Luther King Jr.
9. In February 2022, at the start of the Russian invasion of Ukraine, an attempted coup by pro-Russian rebels sought to take control of several Ukrainian cities and install their own government.
10. Despite the shady nature of the deal, when the Iran-Contra affair and Regan's involvement in it came to light, the American public didn't care nearly as much as it was feared they would.

MULTIPLE CHOICE

1. From 1950–2010, globally, there were an estimated how many coup attempts, with only about 50% of them succeeding?

A. 326
B. 457
C. 179
D. 285

2. Contrary to popular belief, Lee Harvey Oswald's first assassination attempt was not against John F. Kennedy, but who?

A. Major General Edwin Walker
B. Alabama Governor George Wallace
C. William M. Rainach
D. Lyndon B. Johnson

3. One of the main proponents of the 1954 Guatemalan *coup d'etat* (and consequently lobbied hard for it) was:

A. Senator Joe McCarthy
B. Coca-Cola
C. Senator Lyndon Johnson
D. United Fruit Company

4. What does the phrase *coup d'etat*, which entered use in the early 19th century, mean?

A. A blow to the state
B. Justified removal
C. Painful change
D. House falling

5. Before targeting Ronald Reagan, John Hinckley, Jr., originally planned to assassinate which famous person, but was arrested in Nashville for illegal possession of a firearm?

A. Robert De Niro
B. George H.W. Bush
C. Jimmy Carter
D. Jodie Foster

THE CIVIL RIGHTS MOVEMENT

TRUE OR FALSE

1. The Ku Klux Klan was founded in the 19th century and remained active all the way through the Civil Rights movement.
2. The United Auto Workers donated $75,000 to help fund the NAACP's fight at the Supreme Court during *Brown vs. the Board of Education*.
3. Rosa Parks was the first Black woman in Birmingham to refuse to give up her seat to a White passenger, as was the rule at the time.
4. The New York-based National Urban League, founded on 29th September 1910, is the oldest still active civil rights organization in the United States.
5. Martin Luther King, Jr., never supported Malcolm X's push for more direct action, including taking the United States government to the United Nations on charges of violating human rights.
6. Martin Luther King, Jr., was focused only on the struggles of African Americans.
7. The Black Panthers were founded solely as a paramilitary organization designed to protect and empower Black Americans.
8. The Soviet Union reported heavily and favorably on the goals of the civil rights movement, adding to international pressure on the United States government's response to the movement.
9. The support of African American women was critical for the success of the movement, as they provided labor on all levels of the administration of various civil rights groups.
10. Black Panther Party membership mainly comprised of women beginning in the late 1960s, including leadership roles.

MULTIPLE CHOICE

1. Most Confederate statues were erected in what era, and for what reason?

A. 1890s–1930s to support Jim Crow ideals and policies
B. 1860s–1880s to commemorate the Civil War
C. 1870s as people began to examine the causes of the Civil War
D. 1910s as the United States took on more of a policy of isolationism

2. What does the Thirteenth Amendment specify?

A. Slavery and involuntary servitude are illegal
B. All Americans are born inherently free
C. Slavery and involuntary servitude are legal as punishment for a crime
D. Both A and C

3. In response to mass arrests of protestors in Birmingham in 1963, an action was organized that put a new face on the Civil Rights Movement when images of police response were broadcast around the world. What was the protest action?

A. Lunch Counter Sit-In
B. Children's Crusade or Children's March
C. Birmingham Bus Boycott
D. March on Washington

4. Reconstruction (the process by which African Americans, both free and former slaves, were integrated into Southern politics and society) was effectively ended by the enactment of what?

A. The Fifteenth Amendment
B. The 5/6th Compromise
C. The Compromise of 1877
D. The Missouri-Kansas Deal

5. The doctrine of "separate but equal" was established by:

A. *Plessy v. Ferguson*
B. *Brown v. the Board of Education*
C. The Fourteenth Amendment
D. Civil Rights Act of 1875

THE DIGITAL REVOLUTION

TRUE OR FALSE

1. The development of the transistor in 1947 and the optical amplifier in 1957 are seen as the technologies on which the Digital Revolution would eventually be founded.
2. The Digital Revolution originated in the 1980s when home electronics and computers were becoming more common.
3. Built by Konrad Zuse between 1938 and 1941, the Z3 was the world's first entirely automatic, programmable, and digital computer.
4. Despite the move toward automation, industrial workers have had a resurgence in recent years on the job market.
5. The emphasis on speed as the ultimate goal of the Digital Revolution has led to an uptick in the depth of thinking and information available.
6. From their introduction in 1971 to the last version in 1998, the floppy disk went from storing 81 kilobytes to 240 megabytes on increasingly smaller disks.
7. Though they go hand-in-hand, the Digital Revolution had very little emphasis on the notion of "attention economy," or the idea that human attention was a precious and finite commodity that had to be fought for.
8. Internet culture sprang up sporadically as a result of the internet providing easier global communication and has no roots in the "real" world, making it a unique phenomenon.
9. Along with the automation of factory jobs enabled by computer-controlled assembly lines, computers have also taken over vast portions of white-collar jobs such as supervision, management, and information processing.
10. The invention of the solid-state storage systems used in all modern computers replaced the liquid state storage systems that preceded it, which were prone to leaks and even boiling if the cooling system could not keep up with demand.

MULTIPLE CHOICE

1. The Digital Dark Age is about losing information as a result of what event?

A. Massive accidental destruction of digital information
B. The purposeful elimination of digital data
C. World-wide power outages
D. Storage and file formats becoming obsolete

2. What is the act of using digital tools, such as the internet, to cause wide-scale disruption to social structures called?

A. Cyber terrorism
B. Online activism
C. Phone phreaking
D. Cyber activism

3. An act of cyberwarfare involves the what of an enemy nation?

A. Espionage
B. Propaganda
C. Manipulation
D. All of the above

4. The Hacker Ethic shares many principles with anti-authoritarianism, socialism, liberalism, anarchism, and libertarianism. It states ... what?

A. All information should be free
B. Power belongs to those who can take it
C. All power structures should be dismantled
D. Only those with hacking skills should be allowed to have a say in politics

5. A netocracy is a theoretical what, based on internet use?

A. Democracy
B. Aristocracy
C. Economic paradigm
D. Mental illness

ANSWER KEYS:

Prohibition

TRUE OR FALSE

1. True
2. True
3. Bootleg jeans actually originated with cowboys, who needed jeans that could be worn over their trademark boots.
4. True
5. Woodrow Wilson had a large private supply of alcohol, which he kept in the White House until his term was up.
6. It was still perfectly legal to consume alcohol but not to purchase it. This led to a "medical wine" industry, and thousands of doctors wrote prescriptions for it.
7. True
8. Prohibition had always been targeted at the working class, as it was concern about their overconsumption that largely fueled the push for Prohibition in the first place. The rich and upper class were thought to be a "better breed" that could indulge safely.
9. True
10. True

MULTIPLE CHOICE

1. B
2. D
3. A
4. C
5. A

The Space Race

TRUE OR FALSE

1. False. Though there were some mentions in fiction of such a prospect (notably in Jules Verne novels), it was never a real prospect.
2. True
3. False. The United States eagerly snapped up former Nazi scientists, as they recognized that the USSR was doing the same thing and put them to work within weeks.
4. False. Robert H. Goddard was actually a liquid-fuel rocket scientist, but he was mocked in an editorial in the *New York Times* and consequently left the United States. This left the USA without any kind of rocket program for decades.
5. True
6. True
7. False. There were plans as early as the 1960s for a joint space venture between the USSR and USA that were put on hold when Kennedy was assassinated. Plans were resumed in the 1970s, and astronauts and cosmonauts met for the Apollo-Soyuz project in space.
8. True
9. True
10. False. They never protested the accuracy of the moon landing; they quietly and graciously accepted defeat.

MULTIPLE CHOICE

1. C
2. A
3. D
4. C
5. B

Assassinations, Coups, and Plots

TRUE OR FALSE

1. True
2. True
3. True
4. False. His security detail was caught up in a hallway near the kitchen, and it was the writer George Plimpton, retired football player Rosey Grier, and former decathlete Rafter Johnson who wrestled Sirhan to the ground and subdued him.
5. False. There are over 600 documented attempts to assassinate him using a variety of means and methods, including contaminating Castro's scuba diving suit with tuberculosis.
6. False. Though there were any number of plots and campaigns to make various communist leaders lose face, this was not one of them.
7. True
8. False. In 1999, King's widow and children filed a wrongful death suit, and the United States agencies were found to be partially responsible.
9. True
10. False. Reagan's popularity slipped in the aftermath from a 67% approval rating to 46%, the largest single drop in approval for a sitting president.

MULTIPLE CHOICE

1. B
2. A
3. D
4. A
5. C

The Civil Rights Movement

TRUE OR FALSE

1. False. While the KKK had origins in the Civil War, membership dwindled to be almost non-existent until the 1910s and 20s.
2. True
3. False. Other Black women had refused to give up their seats previously, including Claudette Colvin. The confrontation with Rosa Parks gained notoriety partly because she was viewed as more sympathetic to the public.
4. True
5. False. While there was some tension between the two men regarding methodology, they were on good terms when they met in person, and King supported Malcolm X's push to bring the United States before the United Nations.
6. False. King was very concerned with the plight of Vietnamese people and the working poor in the United States. He was planning a Poor People's Campaign when he was murdered.
7. False. While they had less emphasis on non-violent resistance, they provided many community services such as free breakfasts for poor Black children.
8. True
9. True
10. True

MULTIPLE CHOICE

1. A
2. D
3. B
4. C
5. A

The Digital Revolution

TRUE OR FALSE

1. True
2. False. The Digital Revolution originated in the 1950s and arguably earlier when the attitude toward home electronics began to shift and more were available on the market.
3. True
4. False. With automation the need for physical labor has been on a steady decline.
5. False. The focus on speed has led to an increase in superficiality and inaccuracy of information.
6. True
7. False. With the competition for people's attention has come a drop in human attention span in the digitized parts of the world, especially among young people.
8. False. The origins of internet subcultures have their roots in real-world subcultures dating back to the 1960s and the rise of grassroots "zines."
9. True
10. False. The term "solid state" is a bit of a misnomer since the magnetic disc storage it replaced was also solid - the disks were just spinning around in the drive.

MULTIPLE CHOICE

1. D
2. A
3. D
4. A
5. B

CONCLUSION

This has certainly been quite the journey through trivia, hasn't it?

From pop culture to the ancient past, we've covered everything from royal consorts to revolutionary hats. It's been a celebration of pure curiosity and knowledge.

There have been more than a few surprises, some laughs, and probably more than a few things that made you have a good think.

More importantly, this book can serve not only as a gateway to further knowledge, but also to creative gameplay - after all, as we said in the introduction, *The Ultimate Trivia Game Book for Adults* is more than just questions and answers!

Whether you're a seasoned trivia pro or a novice just dipping your toe into the trivia ocean, we sincerely hope this book has served you well.

Made in the USA
Middletown, DE
15 December 2024

66879593R00119